RESEARCH IN TEACHING

RESTY SAMOSA, Ph. D
ELIZA MAE RODRIGUEZ – SAMOSA, MAEd
LAILANIE Q. DELA PEÑA, MEM., MAEd

Published by:
Poetry Planet Book Publishing House
Rosario, Pozorrubio, Pangasinan, Philippines
Contact Number:075-6155455
Email: maritesritumalta@gmail.com

PREFACE

The fulfillment of the research requirement is generally considered to be major stumbling blocks, if not the major stumbling block, among many students, conscious of this widespread difficulty, the author has endeavored to write this book with the ultimate end in view of providing a ready and suitable reference for all concerned. In the preparation, therefore of this volume, the authors have been motivated by one primordial aim of outlining certain essential guidelines - in the form of principles, techniques, and procedures - which he has assiduously accumulated from authoritative books, periodicals, other references on educational researches and thesis writing.

This book was written for the purpose of teaching the rudiments of research and research designing in the simplest and most practical way. Each chapter begins with a tough discussion of research concepts, illustrative examples of research pats and ends with assessment task. It is followed by performance tasks geared to equip the students with the skills in developing competencies in research writing.

This book has seven parts, namely: (1) **brainstorming for research topics,** (2) **identifying the problem and asking the question**, (3) reading on related studies, (4) **understanding ways to collect data,** (5) **finding the answers to the research questions,** (6) **reporting findings, drawing conclusions, and making recommendations,** (7) **understanding ways to collect data.**

This book is an easy-to-read reference with its simple language . It complies with the requirements of the research writing techniques and methodologies for beginners.

The Authors

TABLE OF CONTENTS

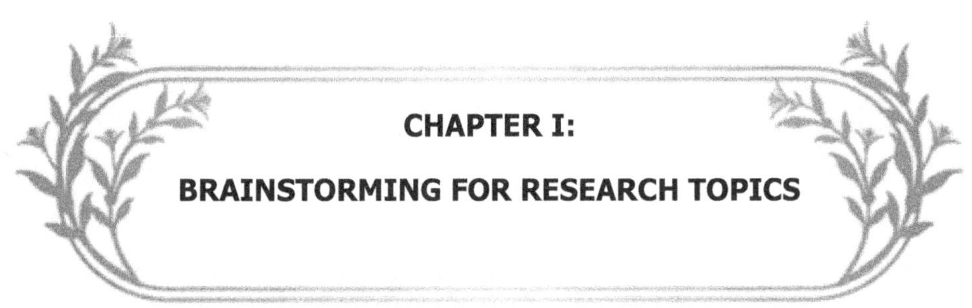

CHAPTER I:

BRAINSTORMING FOR RESEARCH TOPICS

LEARNING OBJECTIVE

At the end of this chapter, students should be able to prepare a plan and a focus on issues and ideas in their respective field.

Research in Teaching

Research is process of finding new information. This knowledge may come through the creation of new ideas or the advancement of established knowledge and theories, resulting in a previously unknown understanding. More so, it entails investigating a phenomenon that has not been studied or is understudied, collecting data to discuss and solve issues, and presenting findings to an audience. Barrot (2017a), the two main purposes of research are to gather evidence and to gain knowledge.

Research may be done inductively or deductively. Research is done inductively if "*works from the "bottom-up, using the participants' views to build broader themes and generate a theory interconnecting the themes"*, it means it starts with analyzing a phenomenon and ends with identifying principles, theories, or processes. In contrast, the deductive approach "*works from the 'top down', from a theory to hypotheses to data to add to or contradict the theory"* it means begins with specifying hypotheses and continues with verifying these through evidence or data. In research, the two main types of analysis typically used are quantitative (deductive) and qualitative (inductive). Whatever analysis or approach you use; the end product of your academic inquiry should be a research paper.

Looking on the, educational research provides a vast landscape of knowledge on topics related to teaching and learning, curriculum and assessment, students' cognitive and affective needs, cultural and socio-economic factors of schools, and many other factors considered viable to improving schools. Educational stakeholders rely on research to make informed decisions that ultimately affect the quality of schooling for their students. Accordingly, the purpose of educational research is to engage in disciplined inquiry to generate knowledge on topics significant to the students, teachers, administrators, schools, and other educational stakeholders. Just as the topics of educational research vary, so do the approaches to conducting educational research in the classroom. Your approach to research will be shaped by your context, your professional identity, and paradigm (set of beliefs and assumptions that guide your inquiry). These will all be key factors in how you generate knowledge related to your work as an educator.

Conducting research in teaching is an approach to educational research that is commonly used by educational practitioners and professionals to examine, and ultimately improve, their pedagogy and practice. In this way, action research represents an extension of the reflection and critical self-reflection that an educator employs on a daily basis in their classroom. When students are actively engaged in learning, the classroom can be dynamic and uncertain, demanding the constant attention of the educator. Considering these demands, educators are often only able to engage in reflection that is fleeting, and for the purpose of accommodation, modification, or formative assessment. Research in teaching offers one path to more deliberate, substantial, and critical reflection that can be documented and analyzed to improve an educator's practice.

Steps in the Research Process

Engaging in research involves following a series of steps or a systematic procedure. This means that you need to follow a step-by -step process to successfully conduct a research study. Avilla (2016) suggested the following steps in the research process to beginning researcher.

1. **Define your topic.** The very first step in conducting research is choosing and defining your topic. Remember that your chosen topic will directly affect the research process, so if you want to lessen your time in gathering information, you have to choose your topic wisely.
2. **Write your problem statement**. Your problem statement is the statement that describes what is to be tested during the entire research process or the general problem or question that the aims to answer.
3. **Make an outline.** The outline serves as the first draft of your paper. Start by writing down all the relevant information you have gathered in line with your research topic. Then logically organize your outline.
4. **Develop a research strategy.** Developing a strategy in conducting your research minimizes the time and effort you will be putting on your paper. This will serve as your guide in setting out your objectives and priorities.
5. **Evaluate your sources.** You must check the quality and credibility of the sources you will use in the study. You may do this by considering the authority (author and publisher), currency (date of publication), and purpose (intention of the author) of the material.
6. **Write and revise your paper.** Check the contents of your paper. Make sure that the contents are in line with your chosen topic and problem statement.

7. **Document your sources**. Documentation of sources is important in any research for it shows the credibility of the writer. This shows whether the ideas or information are taken from other sources or from the author himself or herself.

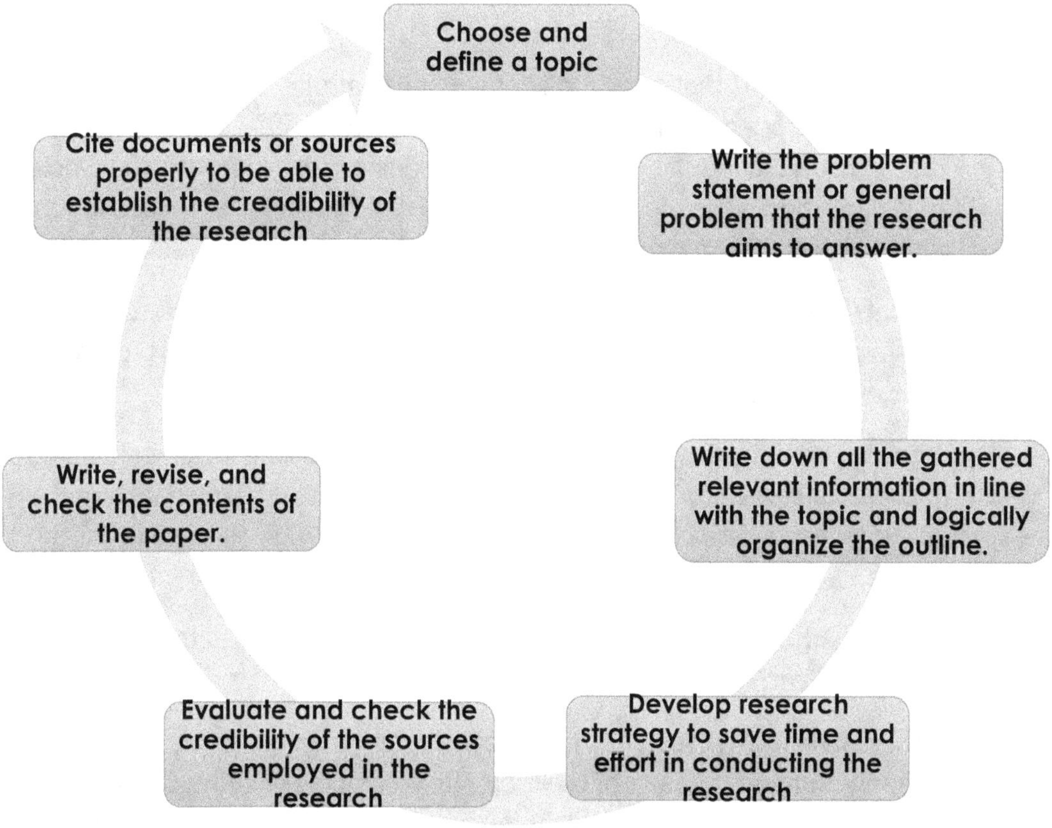

Figure 1: Research Process

Characteristics of a Good Research Topic

All the qualities of a good research topic are based on one factor that is specificity. Every research topic should specifically answer a research question. Choosing the right question and the right research problem is the key to success for every research. Any absurdity, confusion, or loopholes in the research question and research problem will continue throughout the research. One should know precisely what the research problem and its objectives is. Several researchers have determined the qualities of a good research topic. The authors compiled the most basic characteristics of every research topic. These characteristics are necessary whether you are choosing a research topic for your high school research paper, thesis, or any other scientific research. A good research topic should have the following qualities.

1. **Systematic.** It means that research is structured with specified steps to be taken in a specified sequence in accordance with the well-defined set of rules. Systematic characteristic of the research does not rule out (discard, prevent) creative thinking but it certainly does reject the use of guessing and intuition arriving at conclusions.

2. **Logical.** This implies that research is guided by the rules of logical reasoning and the logical process of induction and deduction are of great value in carrying out research. Induction is the process of reasoning from a part to the whole whereas deduction is the process of reasoning from the premise. In fact, logical reasoning makes research more meaningful in the context of decision making.

3. **Empirical/Tangible.** It implies that research is related basically to one or more aspects of a real situation and deals with concrete data that provides a basis for external validity to research results.

4. **Replicable.** Replicability is one of the most important yardsticks for judging the quality of a research. The researcher's presentation and explanation of the system, logic, and data collection should be designed in such a way that the reader is able to replicate the study.

5. **Reductive.** A good research can reduce the confusion of facts that language and language teaching frequently present.

6. **Comprehensive.** A research can be considered good if it has the ability encompass all important parts of the topic into a complete picture. But it should not present excessive detail which may hamper the development of the thought.

7. **Prolific.** It suggests that a good research builds on, but also offers something new to, previous research. It should have the potential to suggest directions for future research.

8. **Relevant.** A good researcher will be able to extract relevant information from large amounts of information. Complete research will have the core information, or sets of core information, which together answers the question directly, and the contextual information, which determines whether or not the core research is applicable to given circumstances. That is, the research topic must be relevant.

9. **Well-executed.** The researcher should also be able to convey the research in an accessible format that is, the research must be easy to make use of.

Guidelines in Choosing a Research Topic

Dela Cruz (2017) enumerated the guidelines can help you determine the viability of topic that you want to pursue and develop in research.

1. Check resources that are related to your topic. If the subject you have chosen has already been extensively written about, or if it is so broad or obscure that no literature exists on it, you will need to narrow it down. You may define the scale, time period, human interaction, and geographic location of your research.

2. It is possible that your topic is so unique that researching it would be difficult. You may want to extend the reach of your discussion. By broadening the subject's reach, you gain access to more detailed resources on your issue. You can only use a limited number of resources if you are working on a very narrow or specialized topic.

3. Avoid topics that you do not have any knowledge at all. For instance, a highly specialized or a very technical subject can be difficult for you to study if you have no background knowledge of it.

4. Researchers must consider the availability of sources. Prior to finalizing your chosen topic, you must assess your research abilities as a student. You may do so by taking your financial capability, health condition, personal qualifications, and trainings as a researcher, needed facilities and time allotment into account. It is important that all of these aspects are considered in order for you to guarantee the accomplishment of your research.

5. Choose a topic, that is not vague, intangible, or debatable or is not easily answerable. Conducting research on the topic should be necessary to produce new knowledge about it or to contribute to the existing literature on it.

6. Choose a topic that is not yet overly written on by other researchers in a field. Always check the library and internet to determine if there is plenty of research already done on your desired topic.

7. Ensure that you have the necessary funds or resources to collect data over a period of time.

8. Consider the resources or budget needed to analyze data or information gathered.

Research Topics to Be Avoided

Baraceros (2019), enlisted the research topics to be avoided. These are the following.

1. **Controversial Topics.** These are topics that depends greatly on the writer's opinion, which may tend to be biased or prejudiced. It is hard to adopt an objective attitude toward controversial topics because these do not lead you to emotional dispute but to an arguable stand as well. Examples of these

topics love and religion where truthfulness depends extensively on your subjectively or on your own personal thoughts and feelings. Facts cannot support topics like these.

2. **Highly technical Subjects.** For a beginner, researching on topics requiring an advanced study, technical knowledge, and great experience is a very difficult task. Highly technical topics involving specialized equipment, complex graphical presentations of things, and elaborate or complicated operations of machines are manageable only by people with technical expertise and practical knowledge in these fields. Topics dealing with mechanical, electrical, computer, or scientific matters are not any researcher but for one who possesses special knowledge and skills in their areas of expertise.

3. **Hard – to – investigate subjects.** A subject is hard to investigate if there are no available reading materials about it and if such materials are not up – to – date. Think that a good research work requires the use of a number of varied reading materials such as books, magazines, or journals from of these reading materials much less, outdated or obsolete ones, proves the presence of a junk research work.

4. **Too broad Subjects.** Topics that are too broad will prevent you from giving a concentrated or an in – depth analysis on the subject matter of the paper. The remedy to this is to narrow or limit the topic to a specific one.

   The broadness of a topic depends on you, the researcher. Considering your abilities, time, and resources, you either find the topic too broad or not. It would be lesser trouble if you opt to undertake a smaller aspect of the topic, rather than to embrace the totality of such broad topic. In your attempt to deal with a broad topic, you tend to diffuse your attention so much so that you make the risk of not giving the required attention to the main topic of your study.

5. **Too narrow Subjects.** These subjects are so limited or specific that n extensive or thorough searching or reading for information about these is unnecessary. A research topic needing so little information or knowledge does not have the characteristics of a good topic for research. Very narrow subjects do not give justice to the true nature of research that demands a discovery of sufficient facts and information from varied sources of knowledge to prove the truthfulness of something.

6. **Vague Subjects.** Choosing topics like these will prevent you from having a clear focus on your proper.

Guidelines in Writing Research Title

A research title introduces the thesis by summarizing the main concept, and it is typically brief and to-the-point (Samosa, 2020a). It might seem that writing is a simple job, but it necessitates more thought on the part of the researcher. Although he or she may have written the study's contents in great detail, researchers may find it difficult to come up with a research title that is succinct and encompasses all of the study's findings.

According to Salmorin (2005) as cited by Gepila et al. (2017), there are some functions that the title serves as it is used in a study among which are the following:

1. It draws, in summary form, the content of the entire investigation.
2. It serves as frame of reference for the whole research.
3. It enables the researcher to claim the title as his own.
4. It helps other researchers to refers to the work for possible survey of theories.

A title does several things: First, it predicts content. Second, it catches the reader's interest. Third, it reflects the tone or slant of the piece of writing. Fourth, it contains keywords that will make it easy to access by a computer search.

In view of these functions, one should consider the following suggestions of Cristobal & Cristobal (2017b), generally, the title should:

1. summarize the main idea of the paper;
2. be a concise statement of the main topic;
3. include the major variable/s;
4. show the relationship of the main variables of the study.
5. includes the main task of the researcher about the major variables under study; and
6. mention the participants and the setting.

Samosa et al. (2021c), asserted the following considerations to be remembered by the researcher in writing research title.

1. The researcher should avoid using words that serve no useful purpose and can mislead indexers. Words such as "methods", "result", "An analysis of" A study of" and "investigation of " should not appear that the title. All these things are understood to have been done or to be done when a research is conducted.
2. In many cases, the general problem of the research or even the specific question that the researcher intends to answer, when rewritten in a statement form, can serve as the title.
3. The title must have 10 to 15 words.
4. If the title contains more than one line, it must be written like an inverted pyramid, all words in capital letters.

Sources of Research Topics or Problem

Research is a venture towards discovery. Before discovery takes place, however, a researcher needs to identify the research problems to begin a study. Figuring out the research problem takes considerable time and effort. What are surefire ways to generate research problems?

The following can help you generate ideas about a good research topic or problem (Bermundo et al. 2010).

1. Prevailing theories and Philosophy
2. Related studies, Literature or recommendation of Previous theses and dissertations
3. Actual problems encountered.
4. Technological changes and curricular development
5. The graduate's academic experience
6. Consultation
7. Specialization
8. Analysis of an area of knowledge
9. Consideration of existing practices and needs
10. Repetitions or extension of investigation
11. "off - shoots" of studies under way

Noticing Spots in Empirical Research

It is important when writing about research to get clear about the difference between research that is adequate, inadequate and research that is partial.

There are four concepts that are helpful in deciding which of these is the case. These are:

1. **Blind spots**. those topics that we 'don't know well enough to even ask about or care about. These are the things, the method, definitions or theoretical approach does not allow to be seen/said. For example, surveys are very good for answering questions such as how many, and how often. They are not very good at probing the reasons why this may be the case. Conversely, a small number of case studies may allow you to build really rich descriptions but does not allow you to generalize to scale.
2. **Bald spots**. Those topics that are repeatedly pursued in research.
3. **Blank spots.** Those topics about which 'we know enough to question, but not to answer. These are the things that are not yet covered by this study. All studies have a particular scope, location, are conducted at a particular time, in a particular context and with particular people and things. there are therefore plenty of other circumstances which the research does not cover. These things-not-covered constitute blank spots.
4. **Bright spots.** Those topics that inspire and innovate research.

Narrowing Down the Research Topic

For most students, narrowing down a research topic makes a huge difference between how they carried out the research while in high school and how they should conduct their research projects in college. Choosing a suitable research topic requires that you work from outside in. Often, you will start with a broader topic and narrow it down to a level where you can establish what you would like to find out rather than only what you would like to "write about." Whether you have been given a general topic to investigate, given several problems to study, or you need to come up with your own topic to study, you should ensure that the research problem's scope underpinning the study is not too broad.

Pulmones (2016), concretized the steps in narrowing down your research topic as follows.

1. Choose a general topic of interest.
2. Add a layer of specificity to your topic through obtaining background information on the topic.
3. Identify the additional specifics of your topic.
4. Choose a particular perspectives or issues associated with your topic and identify the variables you can link with your topic.
5. Write the problem statement.
6. Formulate a working title of the study.

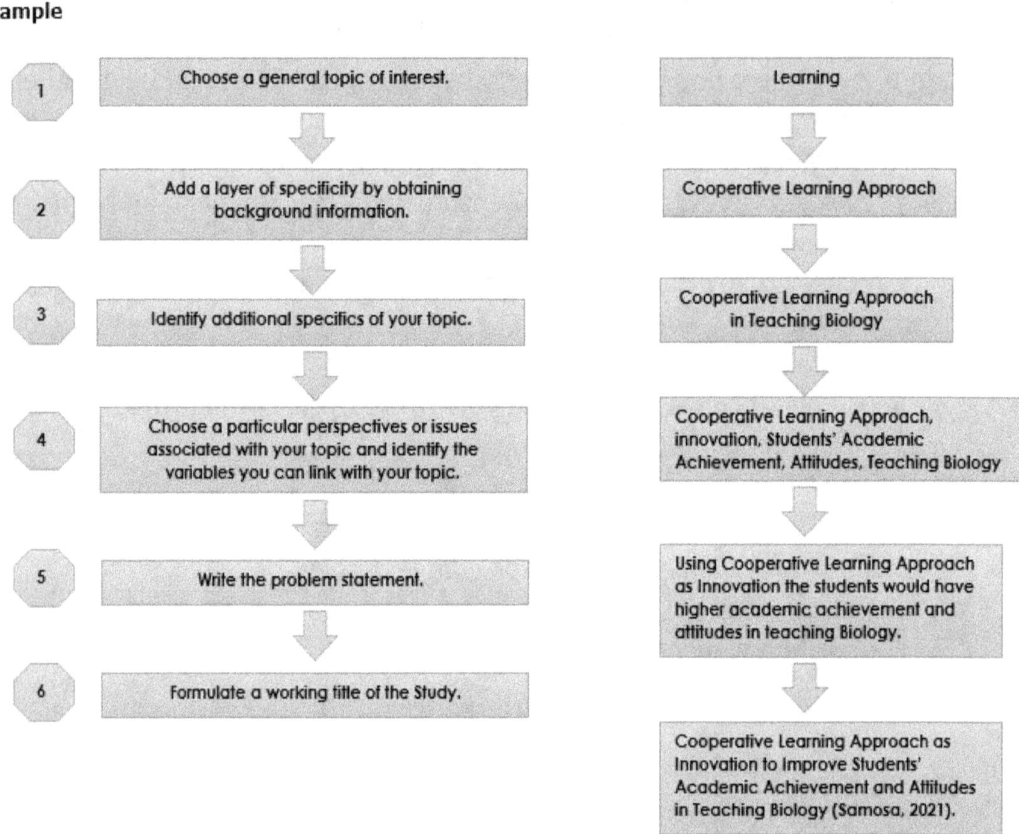

Figure 2: The Flowchart in developing and narrowing down a given research topic.

KWL Chart as Strategy in Developing Research Topic.

One useful strategy to develop your topic is the use of a KWL Chart. Completing this chart helps you identify what you already. **KNOW,** what you **WANT** to find out, and what you have **LEARNED** during your search for background information about your topic. Think of a general area that you are genuinely interested in. Is it in the genre of arts and music, language, education, computer and technology, mathematics, health, business and marketing, environmental science, psychology, or other social sciences?

KWL CHART

General Area of Interest:		
Genre of Research:		
What I know	**What I want to Know**	**What I have Learned**
In answering this column reflects and think of the why, who, what, where, and when questions. **Why** are you pursuing the topic? Why are you interested in the topic? Who are the experts on the topic? Have these experts already published information on the topic? **Who** are the organizations or institutions associated with the topic? Who would be interested in the results of your study? **What** are the problems, concerns, and issues associated with the topic? What advocacies are supported by the topics? **Where** is your topic relevant at local, national, or international level? Are there specific places affected by the topic? When is/was your topic important factor in pursuing the topic?	To answer this column, reflect on your answers to *what I know* column. If you have very little answer to the *why, who, what, where, and when* questions, then your knowledge of the topic is very limited. The next step is to go the library and research for background information on your topic. Remember to consider both primary and secondary resources. Start with the reference section of the library (encyclopedias, dictionaries, manuals, and handbooks). List down explicitly what else you need to know to further describe your topic.	After you have searched for background information about the topic, write your answers on the why, who, what, where, and when questions: **Why:** **Who:** **What:** **Where:** **When:** Remember to add specific details about the topic; identify a perspective or issue associated with the topic' and identify your independent and dependent variables. Write a feasible problem statement. And formulate a tentative title of your topic or study.

Evaluating the Research Topic

To evaluate whether a research topic is a good one, refers to the following checklist:

- [ ] Am I curious about the topic? Can I sustain my interest on the topic all throughout the study? Am I passionate about pursuing the study?
- [ ] Can I answer the why, who, what, where, and when questions associated with the topic?
- [ ] Can I answer the research questions generated by the topic? Are the data collection techniques for this topic feasible and doable? Are there sound procedures that can be used to ensure data collection and analysis?
- [ ] Can I afford to conduct the study? Do I have sufficient resources like time, money, and technical assistance to carry out the research? What are the potential problems in carrying out the study? What plans should be laid out to address these problems?
- [ ] Is the topic valuable? Is it worthwhile to pursue? Is the study of value to me, to me. To my fellow scholar and to the society at large? Would my study give a significant contribution to the existing knowledge? Can other researchers build on or add to my research?
- [ ] Is my study good enough for a class requirement? Is my study practical? Can the results of my study be a source of input for other researchers' cause or advocacy?
- [ ] Is there enough background information to realistically pursue the topic? Are there enough literature that support the findings of the study?
- [ ] Do I have a thorough knowledge of the literature underlying my inquiry? Have I exhausted the available literature pertaining to my topic?

Assessment Tasks.

I. **Direction:** Identify what is being asked in the following statements.
   1. It is a knowledge that may come through the creation of new ideas or the advancement of established knowledge and theories, resulting in a previously unknown understanding.
   2. It is the method of seeking answers to questions.
   3. The process by which the researchers engage themselves in the data they are gathered by reading or analyzing the findings of the study.
   4. Those topics that are repeatedly pursued in research.
   5. It is research approach which starts with analyzing a phenomenon and ends with identifying principles, theories, or processes.
   6. It is referring to formal inquiry.
   7. It is research approach that begins with specifying hypotheses and continues with verifying these through evidence or data. In research.
   8. It means that research is structured with specified steps to be taken in a specified sequence in accordance with the well-defined set of rules.
   9. These are the things, the method, definitions or theoretical approach does not allow to be seen/said in research.
   10. It introduces the thesis by summarizing the main concept, and it is typically brief and to-the-point.

II. **Direction.** Arrange the following chronologically according to what is being needed.
   1. **Research Process**
      a. Develop research strategy to save time and effort in conducting the research.
      b. Cite documents or sources properly to be able to establish the credibility of the research.
      c. Write the problem statement or general problem that the research aims to answer.
      d. Write, revise, and check the contents of the paper.
      e. Choose and define a topic.
      f. Evaluate and check the credibility of the sources employed in the research.
      g. Write down all the gathered relevant information in line with the topic and logically organize the outline.
   2. **Steps in Narrowing the Research topic.**
      a. Write a problem statement.

    b. Identify additional specifics of your topic.
    c. Choose a general topic of interest.
    d. Formulate a working title of the study.
    e. Add a layer of specificity by obtaining background information.

Performance Tasks.

Design and Make Research Plan: Selecting a Research Topic

1. Identify a broad topic you would like to pursue as your research topic? Why is this topic interesting to you? Using KWL Chart answer the why, who, what, and when questions by obtaining background information about your topic. Visit the reference section of the school library or library portal, consult dictionaries, encyclopedia, and handbooks pertinent to your topic. Look for journal articles related to your general topic. Think of key work for your internet search.

2. After obtaining background information about the topic, add a layer of specificity to your topic. Think of a perspective or issue associated with your topic. Is there a seeming debate about your chosen topic? Do you want to come up with a new perspective or definition of a given issue involving your topic? Do you want to clarify something, or perhaps refute, rebut, or provide contrary evidence? Identify the independent and dependent variables that you intend to investigate.

3. State the narrowed topic, making certain that independent and dependent variables are identified.

4. Write your working title.

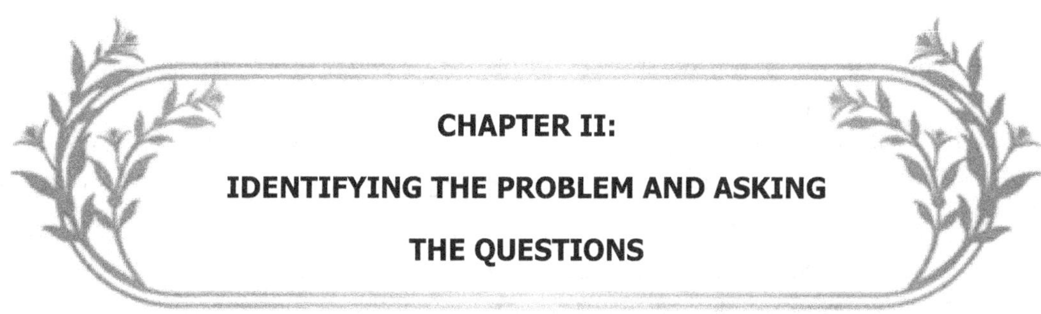

> **LEARNING OBJECTIVES**
>
> At the end of this chapter, students should be able to:
>
> 1. Clearly formulates the statement of research problem.
> 2. Presents written statement of the problem.

Statement of the Problem

The problem is the heart of any research project. Without a focused research problem, there is no research. More so, it will be difficult any research unless a clear problem is initially stated. Statement of the problem states the purpose of the study and clarify various essential elements of research such as the major variables, the general and specific objectives, and the appropriate methodology. This should be in consonance with the research title. The opening paragraph of this part of research paper contains the general problem of the study. It has to be restated with specific details on the participants, setting, and period of study.

Cristobal & Cristobal (2017b) laid down the important elements in the statement of the general problems are:

1. **Main tasks**. They satisfy the question, "what to do the major variables such as to associate, to relate, to assess, to measure, to determine, etc.
2. **Main or major variables**.
3. **Participants. subjects or respondents**
4. **The specific setting**
5. **Coverage date of the conduct of study**.
6. For developmental research and action research, the **intended output** such as an intervention program, module, policies, among others.

Samosa et. al (2020c), elucidated that statement of the problem has two main elements.

1. **The General Objective** - is the first part of the problem where the researcher states the objectives. This is a statement of a long - term objective expected to be achieved by the study. This is derived by the

identification and crystallization of the research problem and as reflected in the title.

2. **Research Questions** - the specific question which are to be answered in the study are called research questions or investigative question and are all in question form. The answers to the research question should lead to the solution of the research problem. Is the objective or purpose of the study observable, measurable or verifiable? Focus on a clear goal or objective. State the precise goal. The problem should be limited enough in making a definite conclusion possible.

Illustrative Example 1 of Statement of Problem.

Effectiveness of Claim, Evidence, and Reasoning as an Innovation to Develop Students' Scientific Argumentative Writing Skills (Samosa, 2020b)

Statement of Problem.

This study determined the effectiveness of Claim - Evidence - Reasoning innovation on Student's scientific argumentation and writing skills in teaching bioenergetics among Grade 11 Students of Graceville National High School from School Year 2019-2020.

Specifically, the research tries to answer the following questions:

1. What is level of the scientific argumentative writing skills of the students after using the CER innovation as described in the following variables?
    a) Claim
    b) Evidence
    c) Reasoning
2. How effective that CER innovation on students' scientific argumentation and writing skills during the experiment?
3. What is the attitude and comfort level of the respondents who have exposed to the CER innovation?
4. Is there a significance difference between the pretest and posttest scores of the students' scientific argumentative writing skills that was exposed to C-E-R innovation?

Illustrative Example 2 of Statement of Problem.

Cultivating Research Culture: Capacity Building Program Toward Initiatives to Improve Teachers Self-Efficacy, Research Anxiety and Research Attitude (Samosa, 2021d)

Statement of Problem

This study determined effectiveness of capacity building program towards research initiatives to improve the teachers' level of research self-efficacy, research anxiety and research attitude among the Faculty members of Graceville National High School from School Year 2020-2021.

Specifically, this research sought to answer the following questions:

1. How may the profile of the novice teachers – researcher be described in terms of:
     - 1.1 Areas of specializations
     - 1.2 Years of teaching; and
     - 1.3 Educational Attainment
2. How do novice teacher – researchers of Graceville National High School assess the capacity building program for action research in terms of?
     - 2.1 research self-efficacy.
     - 2.2 research anxiety and
     - 2.3 research attitude.
3. How effective that capacity building program towards research initiative in conducting action research?
4. Is there a significant relationship between research self-efficacy, research anxiety, and research attitude towards research initiative in conducting action research and the profile of novice teachers – researchers?
5. Is there significant difference in the assessment of capacity building program for action research when novice teachers – researchers group according to profile?
6. Is there a significant relationship among research self-efficacy, research anxiety and research attitude among novice teachers – researchers?
7. After the implementation of the capacity building program, what is the level of the Research Culture Index of Graceville National High School?

Illustrative Example 3 of Statement of Problem.

Cooperative Learning Approach as Innovation to Improve Students' Academic Achievement and Attitude in Teaching Biology (Samosa, 2021e)

A.

B.   **Statement of Problem**

C.

D.   This study was undertaken to compares the application of Cooperative learning approach against Direct Instruction Approach among the Grade 11 Senior High School Students.

E.   Specifically, the research tried to answer the following questions:

1. Is there a significant difference in the academic achievement of the students in Biology who were exposed to cooperative learning approaches from those in Direct Instruction Approaches as measured by a researcher- made achievement - test as describes in the following?
   a) Pre – achievement scores
   b) Post – achievement scores
   c) Gain Scores
2. Is there a significant difference in the attitude of students towards biology after being exposed to cooperative learning approaches and those student in Biology who were taught using the Direct Instruction Approaches?
   a) Pre – attitude scores
   b) Post – attitude scores
   c) Gain Score

Guidelines in the Formulation of Statement of the Problem (Chico & Matira, 2016).

1. The problems be it general and specific should be formulated first before conducting the research.
2. The major problem of the study can be stated by briefly pointing out the objectives, the subject, and the coverage.
3. Specify the sub-problems of the main problems.
4. It is customary to state the sub-problems in interrogative form. Hence, sub-problem are called specific questions.
5. Includes all possible components under the sub-problems of the study.
6. Each specific question should be clear and unequivocal, meaning it must have only one meaning.
7. You should also have advance information on the instrument to be used for data gathering. This will help you prepare the methodology of the study.

8. Answer to the specific questions should contribute to the development of the whole research study.

Classification of Research Questions

Adanza (1995) as cited by Samosa et. al (2021), provide further classification to research questions. These are as follows.

A. **Factor - isolating question -** These ask the question "what is this?" these questions are sometimes called factor - naming question because they isolate, categorize, describe, or name factors and situations.

Illustrative Example 1 of Research Question.

Towards A Digital School Leadership Framework for Schoolhead and The Teacher Digital Competence: Input for School Leader Digital Learning Guide (Samosa; Blanquisco; & De Leon, 2023)

1   How may the school leaders' level of digital leadership be described as assessed by School Administrators and teachers themselves in terms of:
    1.1 Visionary Leadership
    1.2 teaching and Learning
    1.3 professional practice
    1.4 Support, management, and operations
    1.5 Assessment and evaluation
    1.6 Social legal and ethical issues
2   How may the level of teachers' digital competence be described as assessed by school administrators and teachers themselves in terms of?
    2.1 technology operations and concepts;
    2.2 planning and designing learning environments and experiences;
    2.3 assessment and evaluation;
    2.4 productivity and professional practice;
    2.5 social, ethical, legal, and human issues; and
    2.6 planning of teaching according to individual differences and special needs?
3   What challenges do school leaders encountered in the Digital Era of leadership for effective management?

B. **Factor - relating questions** - these ask the question 'what is the happening here?" The goals of this question are to determine the relationship among factors that have been identified.

Illustrative Example 2 of Research Question.

> **Professional Well-Being of Public School Teachers and Their School Organizational Health: Input for Mindfulness-Based Interventions Program (Samosa; Blanquisco; & Mangasat, 2023)**
>
> Do the professional well-being of public-school teachers significantly relate to the school organizational health?

C. **Situation - relating questions** - these questions ask the question "what will happen if...? These questions usually yield hypotheses testing or experimental study design in which the researcher manipulates the variables the variables to see what will happen.

Illustrative Example 3 of Research Question.

> **Video-Based Instruction as A Remediation in Teaching Thermodynamics Among Prospective Science Teachers (Samosa et al, 2023)**
>
> Is there a significant difference between the prospective teachers' pretest and posttest mean scores?

D. **Situation - relating questions -** these questions asks the question "what will happen if...? These questions usually yield hypotheses testing or experimental study design in which the researcher manipulates the variables the variables to see what will happen.

Illustrative Example 4 of Research Question

> **Mathematics Teachers' Readiness, Competence, and Practices Towards International Large-Scale Assessment: Input for School Testing Intervention Plan (Samosa, 2024)**
>
> What school intervention plans may be developed based on the findings of the study?

Criteria for Evaluating Research Questions (Pulmones, 2016).

1. The research question should be researchable. A researchable question is one that can be answered by collecting and analyzing data.
2. The problem implied in the research question should be valuable and worthwhile. Answers to the research questions should have theoretical or practical importance.

3. The research question should point toward the data- gathering procedure to be employed in the study. The research question should provide structure, direction, and guidepost to the researcher as the study is conducted.
4. The research question should specify the samples or participants of the study. These are the people whom the researcher as the study is conducted.
5. The research question should specify the variables of the study. The independent and dependent variables, and the presumed relationship between them should be identified. A good benchmark is to name the variables and how they are related in one sentence.
6. The research question should indicate the methods or data -gathering procedure to be adopted.
7. The problem implied in the research question should be clear. It should be neither too broad nr too narrow.

The Problem and its Background

The first chapter of the research paper, its purpose is to introduce the problem and clarify important variables, its delimitations, and its significance of the field of study. It has the following essential elements:

1. Introduction
2. Statement of the Problem
3. Scope and delimitation
4. Significance of the study
5. Notes in the Chapter I

It should also be noted that the researcher must introduce the different elements to the first chapter by giving a brief description of each element, so that the reader knows what to expect from the chapter:

Illustrative Example:

This chapter presents the different essentials: the introduction, which contains the rationale (an explanation of the reasons to the conduct of the research); the review of literature and statistical foundation; the statement of the general and specific problems; the scope and delimitation which identifies the major variables, sub - variables and the indicators; the significance of the study which enumerates the beneficiaries of the study and the corresponding benefits each will receive; and lastly, the notations.

The Introduction

The introduction situates the research in terms its context and content. This section serves as an introduction to the study, giving the readers a big picture understanding of the topic at hand (Trinidad, 2018). The introduction should provide a "map" of the structure and content/focus of the paper. According to Reyes (2004) the two purposes of research introduction are to indicate briefly what the study is about, and to provide a concise account of the background of the problem and the theory on which it is based.

More so, Cristobal & Cristobal (2017) stressed the importance of establishing the cognitive setting of research and it involves discussing why there is need to study the problem, clarifying the important terminologies for the reader to easily understand what the research is about, and establishing the degree of seriousness of the problem which has prompted the researcher to look for solutions.

The following questions will aid the researcher in formulating the introduction:

1. **What is the rationale of research problem?** This question is answered by sharing with the beneficiaries the reasons why the researcher has decided to look for solutions of the problem. A narration of the researcher's experience that has driven him/her to conduct the study is commonly done. More so, it includes one's personal experience, an article read, a scene witnessed, news heard, a theory that need to be clarified, etc. The research proponent should describe the existing and prevailing problem situation based on his/her experience. The scope may be local, national, or international.

2. **What is the setting of the research problem?** The setting forms part of the delimitation of the problem, as it defines the geographic boundaries of the study and implies certain demographic characteristics. This describes to the reader the place where the research is conducted since the setting has a significant bearing on the variables being studied. In describing the setting, focus on the peculiarity or uniqueness of the setting to make the reader more interested in reading the paper.

3. **What is the basic literature foundation of the study?** This is different from the review of related theories, conceptual literature, and research literature. This part defines or clarifies the terms or variables used in the study. The terms and variables must be clear to the researcher so that he/she can make his/her reader understand them as well. This backgrounder assists the researcher in determining the boundaries of the study. It is derived from different sources. Thus, this part requires the use of various references.

4. **How serious is the chosen research problem?** Why is there a need to look for solutions to the problem? In this aspect, the researcher must see the intensity and magnitude of the problem. When the gravity of the problem has ready been determined, the researcher may act and work on the problem. He/she also looks for statistical or quantitative evidence to assess the weight of the problem.

5. **What is the general objective of the research problem?** This is derived from the general statement of the problem and should be the basis of the enumerated statements of specific problems.
6. **What is the overall purpose of the research problem?** It must be stressed that the researcher should be totally aware of the purpose of the research problem. He/she must know how to the research findings will help his/her classmates or fellow students.

The introduction must only be short and concise. It must be composed of about three to five pages.

Illustrative Example 1 of Introduction:

Cooperative Learning Approach as Innovation to Improve Students' Academic Achievement and Attitude in Teaching Biology (Samosa, 2021e)

There is an ongoing effort in education today among teachers specifically in curriculum development to improve methods of instruction to promote the development of higher academic skills in students. This has led to the development of instructional methods that seek to have the students engaged in the active pursuit of knowledge rather than have the information presented to them orally or through demonstrations by the teacher. Pursuit of knowledge should bear some of the critical features of scientific investigation such as identification of research problems, hypothesis formation, and the collection and interpretation of data. In general, along with. Teaching preparation for public school teachers in science is also a factor in learning. There is only a small fraction of teachers in senior high school that qualified and capable to Biology. Although these numbers have increased for public schools due to scholarship efforts of the DOST-SEI, there is still a need to have programs for them.

The standard of education provided to students by teachers is highly dependent on what teachers do in the classroom. Thus, biology teachers need to ensure that their teaching is productive in preparing the students of today to become good citizens of tomorrow. Teachers should have the knowledge of how students learn biology and how best to teach. Changing the way, we teach and what we teach in science is a continuing professional concern. Efforts should be taken now to direct the presentation of science lessons away from the traditional methods to a more student-centered approach. The science curriculum for senior high school in the Philippines has been designed as to provide students with the knowledge and skills in science, develop thinking skills and strategies to enable them to solve problems and make decisions in everyday life (Montebon, 2014).

In Graceville National High School reveals in the previous mean percentage score in biology in the School Year 2019-2020, are below 50%. The issue of underachievement has been a source of worry to parents, curriculum chairperson and science subject group head, and science teachers. Moreover, based on the classroom observation in biology class have shown that several factors militate against improved and effective academic achievement of students in biology and other science subjects. These include the application of wrong and ineffective instructional strategies in schools. These seem not to help students acquire science process skills that will enable them to understand scientific concepts to excel in examinations, thereby limiting their ability to live self-reliant lives in the society after graduation from senior high school.

Consequently, teachers need to be exposed to effective teaching and learning methods that are learner-centered rather than teacher-centered to tackle the problem of teacher-centered teaching and the low achievement and negative attitude towards biology. To effectively master the subject matter, the learner-centered teaching and learning methods actively involve the learner in the learning process and foster a positive attitude towards the subject. The teaching strategies adopted by a teacher should make learning more learner-centered to promote imaginative, critical, and creative skills in learners, resulting in better achievement of educational goals to improve academic achievement. Therefore, the study sought to determine the effectiveness of cooperative learning approach against conventional teaching on the students' academic achievement and their attitude towards teaching biology.

Illustrative Example 2 of Introduction:

CoSIM (Comics cum SIM): An Innovative Material in Teaching Biology (Samosa, 2021f)

"Rich countries are science-rich and poor countries are science-poor." This statement was made by Dr. Frank Yui, the companion of Senator Emmanuel Pelaez, the "Father" of Science Act of 1958 (Barredoz, 2014).

This is a challenge to all educators to improve the teaching-learning process, especially in science. It is said that science is the backbone of the development of a country and a country with a majority of science illiterates is a poor country.

The Philippines' development challenges can be overcome by committing to science and technology education to help breed innovative ideas, technology transfer and scientific breakthrough for progress. On the other hands, Philippines was joined the Programme for International Student Assessment (PISA) of the Organization for Economic Co-operation and Development (OECD), as part of the Quality Basic Education reform plan and a step towards globalizing the quality of Philippine Basic Education. PISA results revealed that the Philippines scored 357 in Science which is below the average of participating OECD countries. With these it also reflecting the learners' performance in the National Achievement Test, DepEd recognizes the urgency of addressing issues and gaps in attaining quality of basic education in the Philippines (DepEd, 2018).

Consequently, it is a common observation that learning Biology, as a discipline creates a negative feedback to most students in the secondary level. Biology is one of the hated subjects in Science, which students would likely fail completing the necessary requirements and get low performances in both academic and conceptual reasoning skills (Samosa, 2021). To many students, Science learning is never fun, and the process is boring and burdensome; thus, student achievement in this field is relatively low (Samosa, 2019).
Photosynthesis is a central topic in biology education. It remains one of the most challenging, largely because of a) its conceptual difficulty, leading to lack of interest and misconceptions among students; b) the difficulties students have in visualizing the process, or relating it to things they can see, especially when the topic is presented purely as a molecular process; and c) limitations to the practical demonstration of photosynthesis because equipment is either cheap, unreliable and antiquated or prohibitively expensive (Russell, Netherwood & Robinson, 2015).

In the context of presenting science-related contexts and tasks, several different tools have been suggested to directly include intuitive understanding for students and make it more motivating and comprehensible to them. Visual tools are seen as especially important for providing information and embedding it into comprehensible learning situations. One creative way to do this is the use of cartoons or comics (Kennepohl & Roesky, 2018). Comics, whether they are digital media based or traditionally printed on paper, generally belong to the media world of the younger generation. The popularity of comics has been suggested as a cause of both the higher visual literacy and of the decreasing reading skills of today´s students (Tatalovic, 2019).

More so, comics visualize stories, are viewed as comprehensible to students, and also allow teachers to connect scientific tasks with authentic situations taken from students´ lives (Meinhart, & Eilks, 2018).

In response with the educational hurdles encountered, teachers can use variety of teaching methodologies and instructional materials for effective learning. That is why, the researcher decided to utilize the CoSIM (Comics cum SIM) to test the effectiveness in enhancing the academic performance of the students in teaching photosynthesis.

The researcher would like to introduce the application of CoSIM (Comics cum SIM) as innovative material in teaching photosynthesis. CoSIM (Comics cum SIM) are instructional materials that is designed to teach the concept and skills. The vital aim of CoSIM (Comics cum SIM) is to make students master the the concepts of photosynthesis in the easy ways CoSIM are given to the students to help them master a competency-based skill which they were not able to develop during the regular classroom teaching. In addition, once they mastered the the concepts of photosynthesis in easily understand questions and answer it correctly, as a result, better academic improvement is achieved. From the theory of Gary (2012) and Özdemir (2016) Casumpang & Enteria (2019) stated that comics as an instructional material can facilitate students' learning of overarching concepts, such as cognitive development, motivation, information processing and process skills.

With the present situation and existing theories on comics as instructional materials, the researcher tried to test the effectiveness of CoSIM (Comics cum Strategic Intervention Material) as a productive tool in improving students' performances in a teaching biology specifically in photosynthesis, and attitudes of the learners towards utilization of the CoSIM. The study also test the significant difference between the pre-test and post-test in teaching the concepts of photosynthesis that was exposed to CoSIM and the significant relationship between the level of academic performance and the attitudes towards exposure to CoSIM.

Do and Don'ts of Writing of Introduction

Do	Don'ts
present relevant background or contextual material.	avoid presenting results of your analysis in the introduction
explain the focus of the paper and your specific purpose	avoid giving irrelevant information that does not relate to your central idea
define terms or concepts when necessary	avoid giving endless information on the author
reveal your plan of organization	avoid giving summaries of the plot

Scope and Limitations of the Study.

The scope and limitations of the study tells the boundaries and limits of the study. It provides a context by which the study should be seen, read, and understood, it tells where and when the study is conducted and who the subjects are.

This is a phase or aspect of the investigation which may affect the results adversely but over the researcher has no control. Very honestly, he should state this limitation (Dela Cruz, 2011).

Delimitation, on the hand, are the conditions that the researcher purposely controlled. These are the limits beyond the concern of the study (Clemente et al, 2016).

The scope and delimitations of the study may be defined in context and content. Contentwise defines scope in terms of the different aspects or areas specified in the statement of the problems, while contextwise defines the scope in terms of the period covered, the focus subject or inquiry and the place where the research will be conducted.

The following should be considered in writing the scope and limitation of the study.

1. A brief statement of the general purpose of the study;
2. The subject matter and topics studied and discussed;
3. The locale of the study;
4. The population or universe from which the respondents were selected (this should be properly justified or large enough to make generalizations significant);
5. The period of the study.

Illustrative Example 1 of Scope and Limitations of the Study.

Effectiveness of Claim, Evidence, and Reasoning as an Innovation to Develop Students' Scientific Argumentative Writing Skills (Samosa, 2020b)

Scope and Limitations of the Study.

This study focused on the effectiveness of CER framework in developing students' scientific argumentation writing skills of selected of selected grade 11 Accountancy, Business and Management students at Graceville National High School – Senior High School Department. The component of scientific argumentative writing skills was delimited to claim, evidence and reasoning using CER framework.

Likewise, this study discussed the relationship between the demographic profile of the students and the scientific writing skills after using the CER Framework. In addition, it is to identify the level of scientific argumentation writing skills before and after using the CER Framework. Also, it described the effects of C-E-R Framework on students' scientific writing skills in the pre-test and in the post-test. Moreover, it talked about the way teacher-researcher reinforced the lesson in the integration of CER framework in helping the enhance their scientific argumentation writing skills and attitude of the students towards the implementation of CER framework.

This study was conducted at Graceville National High School, first semester, second quarter of School Year 2019-2020 of ABM 11 enrolled in Earth and life Science were made the subjects of the study. To minimize the threat to validity, the teacher -researcher was observed by school principal to check if he was employing the CER framework or not. The observation was made with the use of a classroom observation tools.

Illustrative Example 2 of Scope and Limitations of the Study.

Cultivating Research Culture: Capacity Building Program Toward Initiatives to Improve Teachers Self-Efficacy , Research Anxiety and Research Attitude (Samosa, 2021d)

Scope and Limitations of the Study.

This study determined the effectiveness of capacity building program towards research initiatives to improve the teachers' level of research self-efficacy, research anxiety and research attitude among the Faculty members of Graceville National High School. The respondents of this study were the fifty (50) public secondary teachers composed of nine (9) Senior High School Teachers and forty - one (41) Junior High School Teachers in Graceville National High School. Teachers included in the study as respondents were purposively chosen.

Significance of the Study

The significance of the study in a thesis/ dissertation or in a research paper is a must. For research project seeking for financial assistance by the other agencies, significance of the study should be presented comprehensively in order to convince the screening committee of the importance of the study.

The discussion of the significance of the study is presented either in the inductive or deductive perspective. In an inductive perspective, the researcher moves from the target beneficiaries to the researcher himself, to the people in the community, to the people in the province, region, and nation. Likewise, in a deductive perspective, general to particular, discussion of the importance of the study starts first from the national level to the researcher himself and to the target beneficiaries.

Flores (2016), impinged that the investigator should prove that the study has important contributions in relation to solving the problem and need, bridging a knowledge gap, improving social, economic, and health conditions, enriching research instruments and methods, and supporting government thrust.

Illustrative Example 1 of Significance of the Study

Effectiveness of Claim, Evidence, and Reasoning as an Innovation to Develop Students' Scientific Argumentative Writing Skills (Samosa, 2020b)

Significance of the Study

This study provides useful to the following entities.

For administrators and curriculum Planners. Principals, as key instructional leaders in educational institutions, are responsible for designing and implementing successful learning environments for the SHS students. To achieve this goal, they must be equipped with empirical data to help them make decisions towards the improvement of classroom instruction, student learning and the curriculum in general. In the recent year much promise had been placed on CER Framework, principals and decision makers are found with making choices on implementation Changes in favor of the CER Framework. The research provides the decision makers in schools which such empirical evidence on the efficacy of these practices and thus helps in making these choices.

Science Department of GNHS. For the faculty members of the Science Department, this study provides ample insights in preparing instructional materials and executing innovative teaching strategies using CER Framework. Moreover, this paper shares ideas on building rapport between the teachers and students by lowering the affective filters, hence, maximizing the learning potential. Also, this paper serves as basis in evaluating the present practices of during science laboratory practices.

Subjects of the study. After active participation in the experiment, subjects shall discover, understand and strengthen their facility in Biology specifically in scientific argumentation writing skills. Additionally, after the bearing in mind the positive results of this study, subjects shall develop their sense of pride and confidence, and appreciate that learning scientific argumentation writing skills in biology class is non- threatening experience.

Researchers. Other researchers can use the findings of this study as basis for ongoing or future studies. Furthermore, by conducting similar studies, other researchers can prove or disprove effectiveness of the CER framework in developing student's scientific argumentative writing skills.

Illustrative Example 2 of Significance of the Study

Cultivating Research Culture: Capacity Building Program Toward Initiatives to Improve Teachers Self-Efficacy , Research Anxiety and Research Attitude (Samosa, 2021d)

Significance of the Study

This study provides useful to the following entities.

For the Education Program Supervisor, specifically in Research, this study will provide empirical data on the effectiveness of capacity building program towards research initiatives to improve the teachers' level of research self-efficacy, research anxiety and research attitude among the Faculty members of Graceville National High School. Through acquiring such data, education program supervisor would be able to conceptualize and implement programs and trainings for teachers relevant to research.

For **School Head**. This serves as a guide in designing and conducting teachers training/in-service training. This were increase the supervisory strategies that were help take an action in the teaching-learning areas in the school and the curriculum itself.

For the Teachers of Graceville National High School will directly benefit from the result of this study, this will provide them the opportunity to work on their research understanding and be able to conduct action research to address problems encountered in the classroom.

This study is significant to **schools** because it will equip teachers with necessary knowledge and skills essential in conducting research.

This study is also beneficial to **Students**, especially among the students at Graceville National High School. The result of this study will address problems of students to ensure the achievement of the objectives of the Department of Education in increasing the student's academic achievement.

Future research could also benefit from this study. This research will serve as preliminary framework and as a guide for further studies.

Theoretical and Conceptual Framework of the Study

As soon as the researcher has chosen the research topic, he should look at the theory or principle that link the topic to available body of knowledge. Some schools usually require students to have a separate discussion on the theoretical and conceptual frameworks. Others require either a theoretical or conceptual framework or both. Both of these frameworks provide clear explanations regarding the relationship of variables. The fact that variables can be shown to be associated but does not grantee that the relationship of variables has significance, research study must have a framework as legal basis to describe properly the process of the study.

Zulueta & Costales (2003) ascertain the differences between theoretical and conceptual framework of the study. The **theoretical framework** shapes the justification of the research problem objectives in order to provide the basis on its parameters. It is desirable for a researcher to identify the key concepts that are used in the study for better understanding of the rule of theory in research. It is symbolic construction, which uses abstract, concepts, facts or laws, variables, and their relations that explain and predict how an observed phenomenon exists and operates. An investigation is required to formulate existing theories which link the study because theories are useful devices for interpreting, criticizing, and unifying established scientific laws and facts that guide in discovering new generalizations. **Conceptual framework** presents specific and well – defined concepts, which are called constructs. Its function is similar with theoretical framework because the constructs used are derived from the abstract, concepts of the theoretical framework.

Concomitant, Young (2002), opined that the theoretical or conceptual framework may either be based on theories or concepts. If theories are directly referred to then the research study uses a theoretical framework. On the other hand, if the study is based on concepts, then the research uses a conceptual framework.

Tips in Identifying Theoretical and Conceptual Frameworks (Bermudo, et al. 2010).

1. Although senior high school research may not be theory driven, virtually all studies have an unacknowledged conceptual basis. Concepts (which become research variables) are by definition abstraction of observable phenomena and our world view and views and how those concepts are defined and operationalized. What often happens is that researchers fail to clarify the conceptual underpinnings of their research variables, thereby making it more difficult to integrate research findings. For example, researcher undertaking a study concerned with caring should make clear which perspective on caring he or she adopted.

2. If you begin with a research problem and are trying to identify a suitable conceptual framework, it is probably wise to confer with the broad range of theoretical perspective and are thus in a better position to identify an appropriate framework.

3. It is often suggested that a theory first be evaluated before it is used as a basis for a research project – an enterprise that may be difficult for beginning researchers.

4. In a qualitative study, evaluation criteria for a theory are somewhat different than in quantitative study. In qualitative research in which a theory has been developed, the degree of the theory's fit with the data is considered the critical attribute.

5. If you begin with a research question and then subsequently identify an appropriate framework, be willing to adopt or augment your original research problem as you gain greater understanding of the framework. The linking of the theory and research questions often requires an iterative approach.

6. If you are basing your study on a specific theory or conceptual framework, be sure to read about the theory from a primary source. It is important to understand fully the conceptual perspectives of the theories.

7. It may also be useful to read research reports of other studies that were based on a selected framework-even if the research problem is not similar to your own. By reading other studies, you will be better able to judge how much empirical support the theory has received and perhaps how the theory should be adopted.

8. Once you have identified the appropriate framework, it is important strive on maximal congruity between the theory and its components, the research problem and hypothesis, the definition and operationalization of the concepts and selection of research design.

Construction of Theoretical Framework

See, et al. (2000), identified some methods in developing theoretical framework.

Method 1: Each variable or the concept of the study is linked to a theory or theories.

Step 1. Identify the variables and concepts of the study.

Step 2. For each of the variables and concepts in the study, search for the established or scientifically accepted associated theory or theories.

Step 3. Diagram the theories together with the title of the study with an arrow each from theory box to the study box.

Step 4. Present the textual explanation of the association of the theories with the variables and concept of the study.

Method 2: Integration of relevant studies and other principles into a new theory.

Step 1. Identify and fix the topic of interest to pursue.

Step 2. Search for all relevant studies and concepts related to the topic of interest.

Step 3. Analyze the related literature.

Step 4. Present in a diagram the related studies and principles and the emerging new concept.

Construction of Conceptual Framework

Barrot (2018), suggested some strategies that you can use in developing and constructing the conceptual framework of your study.

1. Identify the key concepts in your study by referring to your research questions or objectives.
2. Search for existing theories that incorporate the same concepts and look into their relationships with one another.
3. Using the existing theories as guide, plot your conceptual framework using a concept map.
4. In case that there are concepts not covered by the selected theories, incorporate them into your framework. However, make sure that you are incorporating this concept into your framework because it is necessary for your paper.
5. After completing the initial draft of your conceptual framework, write a narrative explanation of each concept and how each of them relates with one another. Again, there should be a basis for the relationship among the concepts being incorporated.
6. Check if the conceptual framework is aligned with your research questions.

7. Note that the process of creating a conceptual framework is developmental. This means it may still be refined or changed as you read more literature and look into more theories.

Illustrative Example of Theoretical Framework

Towards A Digital School Leadership Framework for Schoolhead and The Teacher Digital Competence: Input for School Leader Digital Learning Guide (Samosa; Blanquisco; & De Leon, 2023)

Theoretical Framework

With digital and technology continuous influence on learning, knowledge distribution and learning patterns have changed tremendously. Understanding the learning process and patterns in a digital world is important for school leaders to successfully possess digital leadership which underpinned in the connectivism theory.

The realization of learning patterns and environmental shifts was especially essential for educational leaders to lead educational reform such as flexible distance learning. Informal learning played an essential part in teachers' learning and resulted in diverse ideas and resources. Leading a team with diverse viewpoints can be quite challenging for principals.

In the current education paradigm shifts and stated that organizations should provide a connected environment that enabled learners to explore, evaluate, and share knowledge and information as well as construct individual knowledge structure instead of offering consumed or digested knowledge. Creating continual leadership connection was identified as an approach of solving the issue of diversity. The intention of continuous or life-long learning emphasized by connectivism coincided with the innovative objectives of digital leadership.

From this school leaders required in a digital world should possess the capability of leading digital transformation, creating digital learning culture, supporting ongoing professional growth, enhancing continuous organization improvement, and assisting digital citizenship. The dynamic learning environment highlighted by connectivism was a good approach of supporting ongoing professional growth and digital learning. That essential role of connectivism in educational leadership by examining school leaders' experiences and perceptions of systemic change. As implied that continuous learning or lifelong learning was essential for school leaders to maintain the innovative changes. Moreover, teachers needed in time, content-specific, and ongoing support. In other words, school leaders should provide an effective learning environment that should be learner-centered, knowledge - centered, assessment-centered, and community-centered. When providing professional development for teachers, school leaders should consider all learning patterns, including formal, informal, and independent learning. Formal learning, which most people were familiar with, was defined as organizational learning such as district training. Informal learning, described as peers' learning (e.g., interaction and learning with colleagues). Independent learning was explained as individual learning activities. Literature of connectivism learning theory showed that connected, networked, and dynamic learning environments were imperative to enhance and especially expand meaningful learning through communication and collaboration (Zong, 2016). Communication and collaboration were important elements of the connected, networked, and dynamic learning environment. Learning was a dynamic process and would not stop at communication and collaboration. Providing sustainable and on-going support for teachers should be included and considered in digital leadership. For instance, digital leadership was one of the concepts that described and explained the leadership role shift. The effective integration and utilization of technology in schools required support from principals' digital leadership. Affirmatively, that principals' digital leadership not only included getting themselves familiar with technology, but also involved in creating a shared vision of technology and providing professional learning opportunities for teachers. Addressing the skills of digital leadership, the digital leaders offered appropriate opportunities and policies for technology use and resources and they needed the teachers to provide and encourage students as well as parents to involve technology integration. More so, to offered necessary technological support and identified useful technology resources and applications for teachers' future professional training.

Illustrative Example of Conceptual Framework

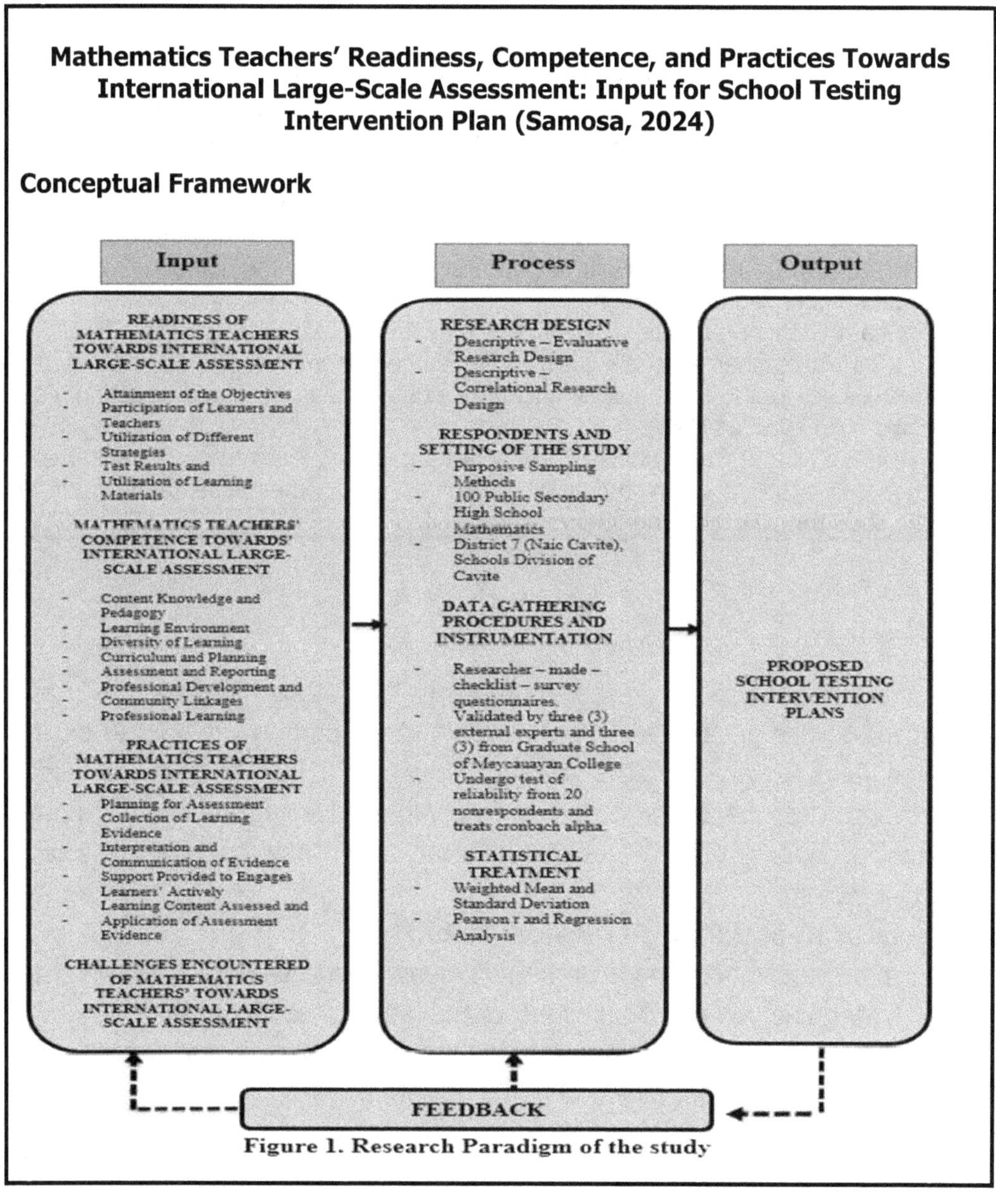

Figure 1. Research Paradigm of the study

>

Figure 1
Research Paradigm

The Input-Process-Output (IPO) model will be used to provide a simple but effective framework for the research design. Scrutiny of the afforest figure reveals that the input frame of the study includes mathematics teachers' readiness, competence, and its practices towards international large-scale assessment.

The first part is the readiness of mathematics teachers towards international large-scale assessment in terms attainment of the objectives, participation of learners and teachers, utilization of different strategies, test results and utilization of learning materials.

The second part evaluates the level of mathematics teachers' competence towards' international large-scale assessment in terms of content knowledge and pedagogy, learning environment, diversity of learning, curriculum and planning, assessment and reporting, professional development, and community linkages. The third portion focuses on the assessment of the extent practices of mathematics teachers towards international large-scale assessment in terms of the following planning for assessment, collection of learning evidence, interpretation and communication of evidence, support provided to engages learners' actively, learning content assessed and application of assessment evidence.

The Process frame consists of the following: Research design, in which the study will be using two methods, the Descriptive – Evaluative Design and the Descriptive – Correlational Design. Meanwhile in the nature of gathering the number of respondents, the purposive sampling design.

For data Gathering Procedures and Instrumentation, the researcher will be using the 4- Likert researcher – made – checklist survey questionnaires. The statistical treatment that will be used in data analysis such as weighted mean, standard deviation, Pearson r and regression analysis.

While the Output frame shows the School Intervention Plans that will be crafted after the result of the research study will be revealed, hence, the results of the study will be the basis for school testing intervention plans.

Hypothesis

Based on the specific research problems, hypothesis is formulated. Hypothesis is defined as wise guess that is formulated and temporarily adopted to explain the observed facts covered by the study (Calmorin, 2010a). Hypothesis guides the researcher to describe the procedure to follow in conducting the study. Hypothesis is important because it tells the researcher what to and how to go about solving the research problem.

Purposes of Hypothesis (Baraceros, 2020b)

Some researchers find hypotheses essential because of the following reasons:

1. They guide you on which aspect of the research to focus on.
2. They provide opportunities to prove the relationship between variables.
3. They give the right direction of the research.

4. They outline your thought in your manner of summarizing the results and explaining the conclusions.
5. They push for an empirical study to prove the existence of relationship of variables and the effects of independent and dependent variable.

Categories of Hypotheses

There are two of hypothesis:

1. **Null hypothesis (H_0).** It is a type of denial of existence of a trait, characteristics, quality, value, correlation, or difference of the result. It is always stated in negative form. The variables are equal; hence, the difference is zero (0). The symbol of null hypothesis is H_0 because all the variables are equal. After the specific problems of the research paper, thesis, or dissertation, the hypothesis is formulated. The null hypothesis (H_0), which is commonly used, is based on specific research problems.
2. **Alternative Hypothesis (H_1).** It is the type of hypothesis which affirms of the existence of observed phenomenon and is the opposite of the null hypothesis because the former is stated in positive form.

Types of Hypotheses

Choosing which type of hypothesis to use depends solely on the researcher. It does not mean, however, that choosing one of the following types of hypotheses make you come out with the best hypothesis because there is no hypothesis type that is superior to the rest (Badke, 2012; Morgan, 2014).

The following are the types of Hypotheses.

1. **Theory -driven vs. Data – driven hypotheses**. A hypothesis that is based on existing theory to explain the relationship of variables and the effects of one variables on the other variables is theory -driven. But if it is based on the findings of previous research studies, it is data -driven hypothesis.
2. **Directional (one-tailed) vs. Non – directional (two -tailed) hypotheses**. Directional hypotheses state the relationship of two variables as well as of the nature or characteristics of the relationship of these two variables. Non-directional hypotheses, meanwhile, state the relationship of variables but not on the direction of the relationship.
3. **Descriptive vs. Causal Hypotheses**. A statement specifying the relationship between tow variables due to the influence of something is a descriptive hypothesis, but if it is due cause – effect relationship, it is a causal hypothesis. True experimental or quasi -experimental research uses descriptive hypotheses.

Guidelines in formulating Hypotheses.

The craft in hypotheses formulation requires you to think of the following pointers (Lapan et, al., 2012; Mc Bride, 2013).

1. Express your hypotheses in a declarative sentence.
2. Support your hypotheses with ideas based on theories, known facts, previous studies of your experience and wisdom.
3. Establish a logical relationship between the hypotheses and the research problem.
4. Have your hypotheses predict the nature of relationship between or among variables.
5. Ascertain the possibility of having some means of testing, analyzing, and investigating your hypotheses.
6. Avoid wordiness by using clear, exact, or specific language in starting the hypotheses.

Illustrative Example 1 of Hypothesis

Effectiveness of Claim, Evidence, and Reasoning as an Innovation to Develop Students' Scientific Argumentative Writing Skills (Samosa, 2020b)

Hypothesis

This study tested the null hypothesis, which subjected to a statistical test at a 0.05 level of significance:

H_o: There is no significant difference between the pre-test and post-test scores of the students' scientific argumentation writing skills that was exposed to C-E-R innovation.

Illustrative Example 2 of Hypothesis

Cultivating Research Culture: Capacity Building Program Toward Initiatives to Improve Teachers Self-Efficacy , Research Anxiety and Research Attitude (Samosa, 2021d)

Hypothesis

This study tested the following null hypothesis, which subjected to a statistical test at a 0.05 level of significance:

H_{o1}: There is no significant relationship between research self-efficacy, research attitude, research anxiety and research capacity towards research initiative in conducting action research and profile of novice teachers – researcher.

H_{o2}: There is no significant difference between in the assessment of capacity building program for action research when novice teachers – researchers group according to profile.

H$_{o3}$: There is no significant relationship among research self-efficacy, research anxiety and research attitude among novice teachers – researcher.

Definition of Terms

It is best to define any key terms in your research study upfront, so that everyone has shared understanding. You will be able to find ideas for definitions by reading around the topic. There are two ways of defining terms in research namely conceptual and operational definition.

A conceptual definition is a critical element to the research process and involves scientifically defining a specific concept (also known as a variable), or construct, so it can be systematically measured. The conceptual definition is considered to be the textbook definition. The construct must then be operationally defined to model the conceptual definition (Serrano, 2016b).

Conceptual definitions are offered in the related literature base. Generally speaking, a conceptual definition should be presented word for word and placed in quotes with the associated reference and page number. In some cases, there may be more than one conceptual definition of a construct.

An operational definition defines a copy solely in terms of the operations (or methods) used to produce and measure it. However, once decided on a particular operational definition for a research study, no one can argue about the definition of the concept for the study. Operational definitions help researchers to communicate about their concepts.

Illustrative Example 1 of Definition of Terms

Mathematics Teachers' Readiness, Competence, and Practices Towards International Large-Scale Assessment: Input for School Testing Intervention Plan (Samosa, 2024)

Definition of Terms

To provide common, accurate, and clear, understanding of the terms used in the study, the following terms are operationally and conceptually defined based on how they are used in the study.

Application of Assessment Evidence. The impact of the evidence collected from the assessment methods and how it affects future instruction and assessments in terms of planning and decision making.

Assessment. The activities and instruments used by the teacher in monitoring the progress and measuring the learning of the students.

Assessment Competence. It refers to the ability of teachers to design, implement, and interpret assessments effectively and ethically. In this study, it is the ability of the mathematics teachers' capacity to select appropriate assessment methods, develop valid and reliable assessment instruments, analyze and interpret assessment data, and use assessment results to inform instruction and decision-making. It is extending mathematics teachers to evaluate the knowledge, skills, and performance of others in a fair, accurate, and meaningful manner.

Assessment Practices. The different methods and strategies used by the teacher-respondents in monitoring the progress and measuring the learning of the students.

Assessment Readiness. The degree of how good and confident the teachers are in conducting distance learning assessments.

Attainment of the Objectives. Targets which specify the knowledge, understanding and skills related to mathematics that learners are expected to have acquired by the end of assessments against a predetermined set of criteria which is clearly articulated levels specifying the degree of proficiency to be attained.

Collection of Learning Evidence. The assessment practices, both formative and summative, are done by the teacher-respondents in determining the learning status and monitoring the learning progress of their students.

Content Knowledge. It is used when referring to the contained thing as an undifferentiated whole. In the study what is considered as content are the parts of a full-length execution of a lesson through a daily lesson plan or the contents of an evaluation tool.

Community Linkages. It refers to the connections and relationships established between individuals, organizations, and communities to promote collaboration and resource. It is expected that mathematics teachers to identify and respond to opportunities that link teaching and learning in the classroom to the experiences, interests and aspirations of the wider school community and other key stakeholders. In this study, it concerns the importance of mathematics teachers' understanding and fulfilling their obligations in upholding professional ethics, accountability and transparency to promote professional and harmonious relationships with learners, parents, schools and the wider community.

Curriculum. Referring to the lessons and academic content taught in a school or in a specific course or program. In the study, an individual teacher's curriculum, for example, would be the specific learning standards, lessons, assignments, and materials used to organize and teach a particular course. All these make up a curriculum.

Diversity of Learning. It is the infinite variety of life experiences and attributes a child brings to their formal learning at school that teachers seek to meet the needs of all learners, so that every student experience success.

Intervention Plans. It is a blueprint for helping a learner build specific skills or reach a goal. In this study it includes a goal, intervention strategy, timeline, and progress monitoring method for alignment of the practices and competence of mathematics towards International Large-Scale Assessments (ILSAs).

Learning Content Assessed. It is the learning competencies and specific learning objectives covered by the topics discussed by the teacher.

Learning Environment. This refers to the diverse physical locations, contexts, and cultures in which students learn. In the study, learning environment is one of the key competences that teachers need to assess to say whether or not they are competent in performing their mandate as public school teachers.

International Large-Scale Assessments (ILSAs). It refers to comparative educational surveys that are widely used to inform policy and provide large datasets for educational researchers that compare skills, knowledge, attitudes and behaviors across different populations and subpopulations of interest which focus in the of assessments on group-level scores in contrast to large-scale testing programs that aim to report scores for individual test takers to use for cross-country comparisons, school monitoring, the evaluation of growth and changes in learning progress over time (reporting of trends), and monitoring progress toward educational development goals.

Interpretation and Communication of Evidence. The practices of the teacher-respondents in: (1) analyzing and making sense of the data collected from the assessment tasks; and (2) reporting the results to the learners and parents.

Participation of Learners and Teachers. The learners and teachers being active and engaged, impacting on curriculum innovation implemented; and feeling of belonging to the attainment of mathematics performance.

Planning. It is the process of thinking about the activities required to achieve a desired goal. It is used in the study as the first and foremost activity to achieve desired results. It involves the creation and maintenance of a plan, such as psychological aspects that require conceptual skills.

Pedagogy. It is most commonly understood as the approach to teaching, refers to the theory and practice of learning, and how this process influences, and is influenced by, the social, political and psychological development of learners. In the study, pedagogy is a vital component in rating mathematics teacher's competence.

Planning for Assessment. The set of guidelines or steps followed by the teacher-respondents in designing and developing the assessment tasks.

Professional Development. It is learning to earn or maintain professional credentials such as academic degrees to formal coursework, attending conferences, and informal learning opportunities situated in practice. In the study, it has been described as intensive and collaborative, ideally incorporating an evaluative stage.

Programme for International Student Assessment (PISA). It is an international assessment that aims to assesses the knowledge and skills of 15-year-old learners in mathematics, reading and science that explore how well learners can solve complex problems, think critically, and communicate effectively that gives insights into how well education systems are preparing students for real life challenges and future success.

Reporting. It is the presentation of honest, credible and impartial information. In the study, reporting has to do with making certain stakeholders like that of the parents inform them about the progress of their children in school.

Support Provided to Engages Learners' Actively. The assessment practices of the teacher-respondents in motivating the learners and ensuring that learning will take place through assessment tasks.

Trends in International Mathematics and Science Study (TIMSS). This international assessment provides reliable and timely data on the mathematics and science achievement of Grade 4 and 8 learners while assessing changes that have occurred in curriculum, instruction, and other aspects of education that affect learning.

Test Results. It provides what the learners have learned what they are expected to learn, such as whether they have met state learning standards which also identify gaps in learners' learning and academic progress.

Utilization of Different Strategies. It is a systematic approach to the process and use of different assessment tools and mechanisms to aide in the learning process that provides learners to participate, connect, and add excitement to the content being delivered.

Utilization of Learning Materials. It is aspects that are taken into account the use of Instructional delivery and design to gain acceptance, implement, and institutionalize a program of instruction of content from the teaching and learning process.

Assessment Tasks.

I.   **Direction.** Suggest some ways to restrict the broad topics. Formulate the statement of specific problem.

1. The school system has five campuses. A teacher wants to compare the academic performances of the students in all the five campuses in all subject areas and all grade levels in relation to the teachers' educational attainment.
2. A school supervisor wants to find out how the academic performance and socio-economic profile of students from all the private schools compare with those of students from all the public schools in his district.
3. A barangay official wants to assess whether the program of the different barangay councils of a municipality are relevant to the goals of all the school in that municipality.
4. A student of anthropology is planning to conduct a study on ethnic tribes in Northern Luzon to find out their practices on marriage, sickness and death, agriculture, fiestas, governance, education, childbirth, religious worship and how these practices have affected their socio-economic status.
5. The President of a chain of business establishments with more than 1000 employees want to assess the level of emotional self-awareness of these employees in relation to their job performance, nature of job and educational attainment.

II. **Direction**. Classify the following research questions. Choose your answer by writing **FIQ** for factor - isolating question, **FRQ for** factor - relating questions, **SIQ** for situation - relating questions, and **SRQ** for situation - relating questions.

1. What is the level of description of the study of senior high school in terms of?
      1.1 review time;
      1.2 place of review; and
      1.3 technique in studying.
2. Based on the findings, what human relation intervention program can be adopted to enhance or improve?
3. What is the difference between the degree of assistance extended by male and female high school students in the foundation day celebration of Dr. Jose Rizal University?
4. What is the relationship of the level of performance of the college instructors to the OJT performance of the HRM students of the Tacloban School of Business?
5. How does the study habits influence the achievement level of the Grade 11 students in their major subjects?

6. How are the following laboratory- related factors be described in terms of:

      6.1 adequacy, usability of equipment.

      6.2 facilities; and

      6.3 laboratory manual?

7. What faculty development activities could be developed based on the results of the study?

8. How does the management procedures applied by the store managers affect the level of customer satisfaction as experienced by selected regular clients of Jollibee stores in the Province of Leyte?

9. What is the extent of transactional and transformational leadership behavior of secondary school principals as perceived by?

      9.1 principal respondents

      9.2 school directors/ supervisors.

      9.3 teachers; and

      9.4 PTA Officers?

10. What part of the curriculum should be enhanced or improved to prepare the senior high school students for the workplace?

III. **Direction:** Formulate an appropriate hypothesis for each of the following research problem.

1. Is there a significant on the mean scores of English taken by K to 12 learners in public and private schools in Bulacan?

2. Is there a significant relationship between Technology Livelihood Education scores and the number of hours of study in TLE of senior high students in public in Bataan?

3. Is there a significant difference in the mean weight of freshwater catfish (*C. Batbatrahus*) cultured in fishpond using fish meal and catfish using bread meal as supplemental feeds?

4. Is there a significant difference in the profitability of pineapple peelings soap and banana peelings soap?

5. Is there a significant difference on the yield of peanuts planted in pots using night soil and chicken dung as fertilizer?

6. Is there a correlation between job-related problems and job-performance as perceived by staff nurses in the city and province of Nueva Ecija?

7. Is there a significant mean difference on the general acceptability of luncheon meat from bone meal of milkfish and goatfish?

8. Is there a significant difference on the educational qualification and socioeconomic status of professors in state universities and colleges (SUCs) in the Philippines?

9. Is there a significant relationship between Mathematics and English taken by Grade 9 learners in a certain State College?

10. Is there a significant difference on the acceptability of fish offal biscuit from milkfish, goatfish, tuna, and sardines?

IV.   **Direction:** On a separate sheet of paper, construct the most feasible or applicable theoretical - conceptual frameworks for the given background of the problem. To help you deconstruct your thinking, identify the variables, concepts, and theories associated or implied in the problem statement.

Short Background

Today's youth belong to what is called the Generation Z. These "young demographics" are being targeted by advertisers. Product are designed and marketed to suit this demographic. Examples of such products are cell phones, laptops, and other technological devices. Members of Generation Z are sophisticated user of technology. They find comfort in browsing the internet and spending countless hours in social media sites using smart phones. It has been observed that today's generation of students have difficulty in sustaining their interest and are unmotivated in reading "straight" text like novels or magazines articles. The medium they like has to be highly interactive or full of graphic to sustain their interest.

A researcher would want to find out how today's members of Generation Z learn and how their preferences for technologies devices can help or hinder their learning. one questions in the researcher's mind is : what is the extent of the agreement of today's youth in social media in helping or hindering them to learn in schools?

Suppose you are to engage in research about today's Generation Z. Using this background information, construct the most applicable conceptual framework for this study. To help you construct your theoretical-conceptual frameworks, fill in the table below.

Variables implied from the background information.	
Concepts associated with variables.	
Theories that can be related with concepts.	

I.   **Direction:** Given the conceptual definition of the following terms, deduce the operational definition. You might need to have additional readings.

Variable	Conceptual Definition	Operational Definition
Aggression	It is behavior that is intended to harm another individual who does not wish to be harmed (Baron & Richardson, 1994)	
Happiness	It is the experience of joy, contentment, or positive well-being, combined with a sense that one's life is good, meaningful, and worthwhile (Lyubomirsky, 2007).	
Anxiety	It is an emotion characterized by feelings of tension, worried thoughts, and physical changes like increased blood pressure (APA, 2021).	
Stress	It is the degree to which you feel overwhelmed or unable to cope as a result of pressures that are unmanageable (Mental Health Foundation, 2018).	
Quality of Life	It is a measure of an individual's ability to function. physically, emotionally, and socially within his/her environment at a level consistent with. his/her own expectations (Church, 2004)	

Performance Tasks.

Design and Make the Problem and its Background.

1. Proceed to the library or search from the internet and look for the research journal related to your working research title. Formulate research questions based on the problem. More so, critique the feasibility of these research questions based on the criteria on evaluating good research questions that you have learned in chapter. Then write a comprehensive introduction based on the following questions will aid the researcher in formulating the introduction:
   a) What is the rationale of research problem?
   b) What is the setting of the research problem?
   c) What is the basic literature foundation of the study?

d) How serious is the chosen research problem?
e) What is the general objective of the research problem?
f) What is the overall purpose of the research problem?

2. The introduction must only be short and concise. It must be composed of about three to five pages.
3. Write your scope and delimitation based on the following:
   a) A brief statement of the general purpose of the study;
   b) The subject matter and topics studied and discussed;
   c) The locale of the study;
   d) The population or universe from which the respondents were selected;
   e) he period of the study.
4. Who are the beneficiaries of your study and what benefits will they receive from receive from the results of your study? Cite at least 3 benefits for each beneficiary.
5. From your initial readings, construct the most feasible theoretical - conceptual framework of the study. What are your variables of interest? What theory or larger field of study are your variables anchored on? What will not be covered by your theoretical-conceptual framework?
6. Give very short explanation of your theoretical -conceptual framework. Deduce the overall goals of the study based on your theorical - conceptual framework. What are some of the hypotheses of the study that can be uncovered from the theoretical -conceptual framework?
7. Define the variables (terms) of your conceptual or operationally.

Rubric for Writing the Problem and its Background.

Criteria	Excellent 16-20	Very Good 11-15	Good 6-10	Need Improvement 1-5
Introduction	The introduction of the study is well developed.	The introduction of the study is fairly well developed.	The introduction of the study is not well constructed	The introduction of the study is badly written.
Statement of the Problem	The research problem is clearly stated and supported by high quality (strong) evidence.	The research problem is fairly well stated, but it provides the evidence that is not as strong it could be.	The research problem is not clearly stated, and it lacks quality evidence for support.	The research problem is not properly stated, and there is no evidence that supports the problem.
Significance of the Study	The importance and relevance of the research is clearly explained.	The importance and relevance of the research is fairly explained.	The importance and relevance of the research is not clearly explained.	The introduction does not state the significance of the study.
Scope and limitation of the study	Scope of the study including the areas that will not be covered is clearly defined.	The scope of the study including the areas that will not	The scope of the study including the areas that will not be covered is	The introduction does not include the scope and

		be covered is fairly defined.	not clearly defined.	limitation of the study.
Research Hypothesis	The research hypothesis is well stated based on the purpose of the study. The statement follows all the guidelines for formulating hypothesis.	The hypothesis is fairly well stated based on the purpose of the study. The statement follows greater than 80% of the guidelines for formulating hypothesis.	The hypothesis is unclear. The statement follows less than 80% of the guidelines for formulating hypothesis.	The hypothesis does not support the purpose of the study. The statement fails to follow the guidelines for formulating hypothesis.
Theoretical & Conceptual Framework	The framework of the research is clearly established. It clearly explains the relationship of the variables with each other. It discusses extensively how it is relevant to the research problem.	The framework of the research is fairly established. It fairly explains the relationship of the research variables with each other. It discusses fairly how it is relevant to the research problem.	The framework of the research is not clearly established. It does not clearly explain the relationship of the research variables with each other. It does not discuss extensively how it is relevant to the research problem.	The framework of the research is not established.
Definition of Terms	The key terms used in the research are clearly defined. The operational and conceptual definitions are clearly stated.	The key terms used in the research are fairly defined. The operational and conceptual definitions are fairly stated.	The key terms used in the research are not clearly defined. The operational and conceptual definitions are not clearly stated.	There are no definitions of terms.
Overall Quality of the Research Introduction	The introduction articulates clear, reasonable research questions given the purpose, design, and methods of the proposed study. All constructs and variables have been appropriately defined. Propositions are clearly supported by the literature. All elements are mutually supportive.	Although a research issue is identified, the statement of the problem is too broad, or its description fails to establish its importance. The research purpose, questions, hypotheses, or constructs and variables are poorly formed, ambiguous, or not logically connected to the description.	A relevant research issue is identified. Research questions are succinctly stated, connected with the research issue, and supported by the literature. Constructs and variables have been identified and described. Connections are established with the literature.	The statement of the problem, significance, purpose, questions/ hypotheses, or definitions of constructs and variables were omitted or inappropriate.

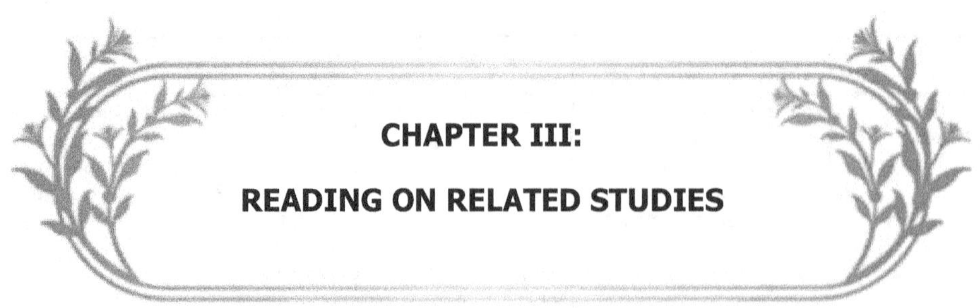

CHAPTER III:

READING ON RELATED STUDIES

Literature Review

A literature review is a piece of academic writing demonstrating knowledge and understanding of the academic literature on a specific topic placed in context. A literature review also includes a critical evaluation of the material; this is why it is called a literature review rather than a literature report (Institute for Academic Development, 2021). More so, it compiles and evaluates the research available on a certain topic or issue that you are researching and writing about.

Importance of a Good Literature Review (Jesson, 2011)

A literature review may consist of simply a summary of key sources, but in the social sciences, a literature review usually has an organizational pattern and combines both summary and synthesis, often within specific conceptual categories. A summary is a recap of the important information of the source, but a synthesis is a re-organization, or a reshuffling, of that information in a way that informs how you are planning to investigate a research problem. The analytical features of a literature review might:

1. Give a new interpretation of old material or combine new with old interpretations,
2. Trace the intellectual progression of the field, including major debates,
3. Depending on the situation, evaluate the sources and advise the reader on the most pertinent or relevant research, or
4. Usually in the conclusion of a literature review, identify where gaps exist in how a problem has been researched to date.

The purpose of a literature review (Ridley, 2012).

1. Place each work in the context of its contribution to understanding the research problem being studied.
2. Describe the relationship of each work to the others under consideration.
3. Identify new ways to interpret prior research.
4. Reveal any gaps that exist in the literature.
5. Resolve conflicts amongst seemingly contradictory previous studies.
6. Identify areas of prior scholarship to prevent duplication of effort.
7. Point the way in fulfilling a need for additional research.
8. Locate your own research within the context of existing literature.

Types of Literature Reviews

Literature reviews are designed to provide an overview of sources the researcher has explored while researching a particular topic and to demonstrate to the readers how the research fits within a larger field of study. The following are the basic types of literature review:

1. **Narrative literature review.** critiques the literature and summarizes the body of a literature. Narrative review also draws conclusions about the topic and identifies gaps or inconsistencies in a body of knowledge. You need to have a sufficiently focused research question to conduct a narrative literature review.

2. **Systematic literature.** review requires more rigorous and well-defined approach compared to most other types of literature review. Systematic literature review is comprehensive and details the timeframe within which the literature was selected. Systematic literature review can be divided into two categories: meta-analysis and meta-synthesis. When you conduct meta-analysis, you take findings from several studies on the same subject and analyze these using standardized statistical procedures. In meta-analysis patterns and relationships are detected and conclusions are drawn. Meta-analysis is associated with deductive research approach.

   Meta-synthesis, on the other hand, is based on non-statistical techniques. This technique integrates, evaluates and interprets findings of multiple qualitative research studies. Meta-synthesis literature review is conducted usually when following inductive research.

3. **Argumentative literature review.** as the name implies, examines literature selectively in order to support or refute an argument, deeply imbedded assumption, or philosophical problem already established in the literature. It

should be noted that a potential for bias is a major shortcoming associated with argumentative literature review.

4. **Integrative literature review.** It reviews, critiques, and synthesizes secondary data about research topic in an integrated way such that new frameworks and perspectives on the topic are generated. If your research does not involve primary data collection and data analysis, then using integrative literature review will be your only option.

5. **Theoretical literature review** focuses on a pool of theory that has accumulated in regard to an issue, concept, theory, phenomena. Theoretical literature reviews play an instrumental role in establishing what theories already exist, the relationships between them, to what degree the existing theories have been investigated, and to develop new hypotheses to be tested.

6. **Methodological Review**. A review does not always focus on what someone said [content], but how they said it [method of analysis]. This approach provides a framework of understanding at different levels (i.e. those of theory, substantive fields, research approaches and data collection and analysis techniques), enables researchers to draw on a wide variety of knowledge ranging from the conceptual level to practical documents for use in fieldwork in the areas of ontological and epistemological consideration, quantitative and qualitative integration, sampling, interviewing, data collection and data analysis, and helps highlight many ethical issues which we should be aware of and consider as we go through our study.

Literature Review Organization

1. **Chronological.** If your review follows the chronological method, you could write about the materials according to when they were published. This approach should only be followed if a clear path of research building on previous research can be identified and that these trends follow a clear chronological order of development.

2. **By Publication.** Order your sources by publication chronology, then, only if the order demonstrates a more important trend. For instance, you could order a review of literature on environmental studies of brown fields if the progression revealed, for example, a change in the soil collection practices of the researchers who wrote and/or conducted the studies.

3. **Thematic (conceptual categories).** Thematic reviews of literature are organized around a topic or issue, rather than the progression of time. However, progression of time may still be an important factor in a thematic review. The only difference here between a "chronological" and a "thematic" approach is what is emphasized the most. Note however that more authentic

thematic reviews tend to break away from chronological order. A review organized in this manner would shift between time periods within each section according to the point made.

4. **Methodological.** A methodological approach focuses on the methods utilized by the researcher.

Writing Your Literature Review

Once you have settled on how to organize your literature review, you are ready to write each section. When writing your review, keep in mind these issues.

1. **Use Evidence.** A literature review section is, in this sense, just like any other academic research paper. Your interpretation of the available sources must be backed up with evidence [citations] that demonstrates that what you are saying is valid.

2. **Be Selective.** Select only the most important points in each source to highlight in the review. The type of information you choose to mention should relate directly to the research problem, whether it is thematic, methodological, or chronological. Related items that provide additional information but that are not key to understanding the research problem can be included in a list of further readings.

3. **Use Quotes Sparingly.** Some short quotes are okay if you want to emphasize a point, or if what an author stated cannot be easily paraphrased. Sometimes you may need to quote certain terminology that was coined by the author, not common knowledge, or taken directly from the study. Do not use extensive quotes as a substitute for your own summary and interpretation of the literature.

4. **Summarize and Synthesize.** Remember to summarize and synthesize your sources within each thematic paragraph as well as throughout the review. Recapitulate important features of a research study, but then synthesize it by rephrasing the study's significance and relating it to your own work.

5. **Keep Your Own Voice.** While the literature review presents others' ideas, your voice [the writer's] should remain front and center. For example, weave references to other sources into what you are writing but maintain your own voice by starting and ending the paragraph with your own ideas and wording.

6. **Use Caution When Paraphrasing.** When paraphrasing a source that is not your own, be sure to represent the author's information or opinions accurately and in your own words. Even when paraphrasing an author's work, you still must provide a citation to that work.

Common Mistakes to Avoid in Writing Literature Review.

These are the most common mistakes made in reviewing literature.
1. Sources in your literature review do not clearly relate to the research problem;
2. You do not take sufficient time to define and identify the most relevant sources to use in the literature review related to the research problem;
3. Relies exclusively on secondary analytical sources rather than including relevant primary research studies or data;
4. Uncritically accepts another researcher's findings and interpretations as valid, rather than examining critically all aspects of the research design and analysis.
5. Does not describe the search procedures that were used in identifying the literature to review;
6. Reports isolated statistical results rather than synthesizing them in chi-squared or meta-analytic methods; and,
7. Only includes research that validates assumptions and does not consider contrary findings and alternative interpretations found in the literature.

Parts of Literature Review

Most lit reviews use a basic introduction-body-conclusion structure; if your lit review is part of a larger paper, the introduction and conclusion pieces may be just a few sentences while you focus most of your attention on the body. If your lit review is a standalone piece, the introduction and conclusion take up more space and give you a place to discuss your goals, research methods, and conclusions separately from where you discuss the literature itself.

1. **Introduction.**
    a) An introductory paragraph that explains what your working topic and thesis is
    b) A forecast of key topics or texts that will appear in the review.
    c) Potentially, a description of how you found sources and how you analyzed them for inclusion and discussion in the review (more often found in published, standalone literature reviews than in lit review sections in an article or research paper)
2. **Body.**
    a) Summarize and synthesize: Give an overview of the main points of each source and combine them into a coherent whole.
    b) Analyze and interpret: Don't just paraphrase other researchers – add your own interpretations where possible, discussing the significance of findings in relation to the literature as a whole.

   c) Critically Evaluate: Mention the strengths and weaknesses of your
      sources.
   d) Write in well-structured paragraphs: Use transition words and topic
      sentence to draw connections, comparisons, and contrasts.
3. **Conclusion.**
   a) Summarize the key findings you have taken from the literature and
      emphasize their significance.
   b) Connect it back to your primary research question.

Literature Review Strategies

The following are brief descriptions of techniques that you might use in your literature review. Choose the approaches that are the most pertinent to your rhetorical situation.

1. **Summary.** Briefly state the argument and main points of relevant research.
2. **Synthesis.** Combine ideas in order to form an integrated theory or system through critical evaluation, compare/contrast, etc.
3. **Analysis.** Closely examine the elements or structure of the research and interpret through the lens of the field.
4. **Evaluation.** Assess the research based on criteria you choose, state, and explain. Support your evaluation with research.

Thesis Statement: Service-learning programs implemented in American undergraduate universities since 2000 have not only proven beneficial for the individuals or organizations being served but also for the participating students by offering opportunities for academic, emotional, and social growth.

Prior studies have identified many benefits for educational institutions from service-learning programs. These benefits include positive perceptions of the university by the community (Miron & Moely, 2006), enhanced student retention rates (Eyler et al., 2001), positive teaching and learning outcomes such as greater student involvement and participation in class (Caruso et al., 2007), and increased opportunities for meaningful research and scholarly activities (Strand et al., 2003).

In this study and related research, the individuals serving are university students who are collaborating with the community partner. The studied benefits to individuals serving include cultural awareness sharing (Crabtree, 2008), as well as networking opportunities and application of classroom learning to real-world issues (Bowen et al., 2009). Ultimately, service-learning stimulates student learning and engages students in their surrounding communities. Service learning creates new goals for students such as personal development, career development, moral development, academic achievement, and "reflective civic participation" (Lamb et al., 1998). These types of projects allow students to utilize material learned in the classroom to improve societal conditions.

Integrating concepts and theories learned in the classroom with everyday life makes students more capable of highlighting the importance of each course. Additionally, material learned in business courses can be applied to benefit the community through a variety of tangible services, such as business planning or marketing new programs. Service learning is an excellent way for students to apply their course lessons to real-world situations and concurrently benefit the community.

Summary of key research

Evaluation and application to thesis/topic

Analysis and Synthesis

Citation Styles

A **citation** is a reference to a source used in your research. It is how you give credit to the author for their creative and intellectual works that you referenced as support for your research. Generally, citations should include author's name, date, publisher information, journal information and/or DOI (Digital Object Identifier).

Citation styles are the formal way that citation information is formatted. It dictates what information is included, how it is ordered as well as punctuation and other formatting. There are many different styles and each mandate order of appearance of information (such as publication date, title, and page numbers following the author's name etc), conventions of punctuation, use of italics (and underlining for emphasis) that are particular to their style.

There are many different ways of citing resources from your research. The citation style sometimes depends on the academic discipline involved and sometimes depends on the publisher/ place of publishing.

Importance of a Citing Sources

Citations document for your readers where you obtained your material, provide a means of critiquing your study based on the sources you used, and create an opportunity to obtain information about prior studies of the research problem under investigation. The act of citing sources is also your best defense against allegations of plagiarism.

Citing the works of others is important because:

1. **Proper citation allows readers to locate the materials you used**. Citations to sources helps readers expand their knowledge on a topic. One of the most effective strategies for locating authoritative, relevant sources about a topic is to review footnotes or references from known sources ["citation tracking"].

2. **Citing other people's words and ideas demonstrates that you have conducted a thorough review of the literature on your topic** and, therefore, you are reporting your research from an informed and critically engaged perspective. The list of sources used increases your credibility as the author of the work.

3. **Other researcher's ideas can be used to reinforce your arguments**. In many cases, another researcher's arguments can act as the primary context from which you can emphasize the significance of your study and to provide supporting evidence about how you addressed the "So What?" question.

4. **The ideas of other researchers can be used to explain reasons for alternative approaches**. If you disagree with a researcher's ideas or you believe there is a gap in understanding the research problem, your citations can serve as sources from which to argue an alternative viewpoint or the need to pursue a different course of action.

5. **Just as the ideas of other researchers can bolster your arguments, they can also detract from your credibility if their research is challenged**. Properly citing sources prevents your reputation from being tarnished if the facts or ideas of those cited are proven to be inaccurate or off-

base. It prevents readers from concluding that you ignored or dismissed the findings of others, even if they are disputed.

6. **Ideas are considered intellectual property and there can be serious repercussions if you fail to cite where you got an idea from**. In academe and the professional world, failure to cite other people's intellectual property ruins careers and reputations and can result in legal action. Citing sources as a student in college will help you get in the habit of acknowledging and properly citing the work of others.

In any academic writing, you are required to identify which ideas, facts, thoughts, and concepts are yours and which are derived from the research and work of others. Whether you summarize, paraphrase, or use direct quotes, if it is not your original idea, the source must be acknowledged. The only possible exception to this rule is information that is considered to be a commonly known fact. Appreciate, however, that any "commonly known fact" is culturally constructed and shaped by social and aesthetical biases. If you are in doubt about whether or not a fact is common knowledge, protect yourself from an allegation of plagiarism and provide a supporting citation, or ask your research teacher for clarification about how a factual statement should be cited.

Different Styles of Research Writing

In research writing, there are many different style guides that are followed by researcher. However, the three most common styles followed at present are the Modern Language Association (MLA) Style, American Psychological Association (APA) Style, and Chicago Style or Turabian.
Modern Language Association (MLA) Style
The Modern Language Association (MLA) Style is an American professional organization for scholar of Literature based in New York City. It published the MLA stylebook titled MLA Style Manual and Guide to Scholar Publishing with its first edition printed in 1985 and its third edition in 2008. The MLA began in 1883 at Purdue University as discussion group for literature and modern language. Today, several regional associations compose the MLA.

Formatting a Paper Using the MLA Style
By Peter Gallagher and Brian Scott

1. **Alignment** - Align the text flush left. If your word processor, such as Microsoft Word has a "full justify" setting which spread the text and aligns it both left and right, do not use it. Leave the next ragged on the right side.

2. **Binding** - MLA Style calls for binding the pages with a simple paper clip or spring clip. Do not use a staple or other permanent binding system, unless your instructor requests it.

3. **Endnotes and footnotes** - You may use endnotes with Style, but they should be used to further explain a term or a complex idea beyond what you are able to include in the main text. Endnotes and footnotes should not be cited sources. Save those for the "Works Cited" page.

4. **Font** - MLA Style calls for a 12 - point font size, along with an easily readable font such as Times New Roman.

5. **Headings** - In MLA Style, headings and subheads that break up the text are optional. Check with your instructor before using them.

6. **Indentions** - You will need to indent the first line of any paragraph by one - half inch from the left margin. If your instructor before using them.

7. **Font** - MLA Style calls for a 12 - point font size, along with an easily readable font such as Times New Roman.

8. **Headings** - In MLA Style, headings and subheads that break up the text are optional. Check with your instructor before using them.

9. **Indentions** - You will need to indent the first line of any paragraph by one - half inch from the left margin.

10. **Italics** - You should use italics for titles of longer works. MLA Style also allows. MLA Style also allows the use of italics within the body of the text for particular word or phrases but use such items sparingly.

11. **Margin** - All four sides of the MLA paper - top, bottom, right, and left - requires a margin of 1 inch. The only items that should appear outside the margins are the page numbers.

12. **Page numbering** - Place the page number in upper of every page. Use Arabic numerals for the page numbers. The page number should one - half inch from the top of the paper and even with the margin (1 inch from the edge of the paper). If you choose to use an optional title page, you should not number it. If you choose not to create a separate title page, instead including the title and other relevant information on the first page of the main text, you must use "1" as the number of that page.

13. **Spacing -** You will need to double space all of the text within the paper, except in special circumstances as directed by your instructor. All quotations, notes and list of works cited should be double - spaced.

14. **Title** - MLA Style does not require a separate title page. You can include the information used for the title on the first page of the paper and begin the paper's main text on the same page. All text should be double - spaced on the first page. You can place the page number in the upper right corner. In the upper left corner, flush left, and beginning at the margins, include your name, the instructor's name, the course, and the date. Then, center the text for the title, mixing uppercase and lowercase letters. If you choose to skip the

separate title page, you can begin the main text immediately after the title page; you can begin the main text immediately after the title text.

15. **Underlining** - with the third edition of the MLA Style manual, the new guidelines have eliminated the use of underlining. Now, italicize all published works, rather than underlining.

American Psychological Association (APA)

The American Psychological Association or (APA) developed its own uniform style of formatting written works. Originally, the resulting style book was provided to their associates as guide for composing scientific publications, article, handbooks, journals, and the like for the organization. It was in 1929 when the original APA guidelines were featured in a magazine write - up. It was only in 1559 when an official APA style manual became publicly available. Because of the practicability it brings, many education institutions use the APA style as the standard for writing research papers.

Formatting a Paper Using the APA Style
By Peter Gallagher and Brian Scott

1. **Abbreviations** - avoid using abbreviation in your paper. However; if you need to use an abbreviation or acronym that is recognized in your language and you can find it in the dictionary then you can use it.

2. **Hyphenation** - Do not separate and hyphenate words at the end f a line. Rather, leave one time slightly short and put the complete word on the next line; otherwise, proceed a couple of characters past the right margin to adjust the complete word on line.

3. **Indention** - Indent paragraph within the primary text of the paper one half inch if using a word processing program or indent five to seven spaces in if typing on a typewriter, however do not indent in these unique circumstances: the abstract, block quotations, figure captions, notes, reference list entries, table titles or headings.

4. **Margins** - use 1-inch margins on all four sides of the paper: top, bottom, right, and left. Old rules required 1.5 - inch margins, but these rules are now obsolete.

5. **Page numbering** - Number nearly every page in the paper, including the title page. Put the number in the upper - right corner of the page and use only Arabic numbers. Put the number "1" on the title page and the number "2" on the abstract page. Begin the main body of the text on page number "3". Do not number pages that consist of only statistics or illustration.

6. **Paper type** - Use regular white, 20 - pound bond paper that has measurements of 8.5 by 11 inches. If printing from a computer, use an inkjet or laser printer to print the paper; if you use a tractor - feed printer, make sure to tear off the pinhole border from the sides of the paper.

7. **Parentheses** - Aim to restrict parentheses to separate or divide items that are structurally independent, such as listing a number or illustration that is associated with a sentence. If you are enclosing a full sentence in parentheses, position the punctuation inside the parentheses. If you are enclosing only a piece of a sentence inside parentheses, then place the punctuation outside the parentheses.

8. **Punctuation** - In most cases, use single space after all common punctuation mark, such as periods, commas, colons, and semicolons. There are three exceptions to this norm:

     a. do not use a space after periods inside an abbreviation, such as when writing U.S for United States;

     b. do not use a space after a colon in a ratio such as 4:7; and

     c. Some professors like the outdated rule of using two spaces after periods that end sentences. If you are using Courier or another mono-space font, APA Style does permit two spaces between sentences, although one space is recommended.

9. **Short title** - A short title is a two - or three - word introduction of the main title. Put it on every page in the top right corner, except for pages that consist of only numbers or illustrations. The short title should appear slightly to the left of the page number.

10. **Slash mark** - Do not use slash marks in your paper. For instance, rather than writing "blue and or purple", it is better to write, "blue, purple or both".

11. **Spacing** - Use double spacing throughout the whole paper, unless your professor expressly asks for single spacing in specific situation such as with block quotation.

12. **Text alignment -** Always format the text flush left. Do not use the "full justify" features on your word processor's toolbar because this will spread the text fully across the paper and align sentences both left and right.

13. **Title** - center the title on the title page, creating a combination of uppercase and lowercase letter. If the title is long enough to warrant a second line, double space between the lines. After the title, include your name, followed by the college that you attend. If you do not belong to college, you can substitute the city and state. Double space between each line on the title page. Put the number "1" in the upper right corner of the title page.

14. **Typeface** - If using a word processor like MS Word, opt for a Serif font, such as Times New Roman. Use text in a 10 or 12 - point size.

Chicago Style and Turabian Style

The University of Chicago Press manages the standards and rules for the Chicago style. The principal handbook entitled *The Chicago Manual of Style*, is sometimes shorted to "CMS" or "CMOS." The University of Chicago Press produced the original Chicago Style Manual in 1906.

Chicago Style also has a second handbook entitled *A Manual for Writer of Term Papers, Theses, and Dissertations*, which is written by Kate Turabian, a senior disquisition assistant at the University of Chicago. She develops the Turabian manual as a supplement to the Chicago Style manual.

One will often hear that the Turabian Style and Chicago Style are the same style because they have identical but slightly refined rules. The two styles are nearly similar that professors often refer to them in combination. Turabian Style permits the use of footnotes for citing sources, which splits it from other styles on writing formal papers. Papers that adhere to Chicago Style typically are fewer formal papers and not designed for publication. However, Chicago Style is versatile enough to deal with any style of paper, including papers, essays, repots, theses, or dissertations.

Formatting a Paper Using the Chicago or Turabian Style
By Peter Gallagher and Brian Scott

1. **Abbreviating** - Abbreviations are more acceptable in academic papers than they were ten years ago. If you need to abbreviate, use the customary, well known ones such as "AIDS" or "ADHD." One exception is not to abbreviate phrases of ranges, such as "yards" or "miles." If your abbreviation contains two periods, such as "U.K." or "N.J."; do not include a space after the first period.
2. **Text alignment** - Justify all text to the left (excluding indentions), but you may also use ragged right justification or use full (block) justification. If you opt full justification, you must make sure that you space minimally between words and you hyphenate text properly and moderately. Your word processing software should allow you to comply wuth these two guidelines for full justification, except if you have many mutli-syllable big words in your paper.
3. **Capitalizing** - Use "headline - style" capitalize all words aside from articles, some prepositions, and conjunctions. Use "sentence - style" capitalization to capitalize only the first word, a word following a colon, and proper nouns.
4. **White out** - You can apply white correcting fluid to mask black dots and stray spots on the final paper.
5. **Date format** - You can use either one of two date formats: "23 April 2012" (day, month, year) or "April 23, 2012" (month, date, year). When you choose

one format, you must stick with the same one throughout your paper. Do not use a combination of the two.

6. **Font style** - Always use a Serif font, such as Times New Roman, for the primary text of your paper. Use a font size between 10 - and 12 - point sizes. A computer - generated font is exceedingly better than any mechanical type because it creates perfect italicized and solid boldface text.

7. **When to hyphenate** - You can hyphenate words at the end of a line in your primary text, but you should avoid hyphenating words at the end two successive lines.

8. **When to indent text** - Indent paragraph within the primary text f your paper by one and a half inch or approximately 5 to 8 spaces. Chicago Style does not mandate a precise measure of indention, but you must use the same space of indention in your entire paper.

9. **Margin sizes** - Use the standard 1 - inch margin on all four sides of your paper. However, if you are going to bind your paper on the left side, then you can use a wider left margin.

10. **Number** - Always spell out and use words for each number, one through one hundred. For number exceeding 100, use basic numerals. Adhere to these exceptions :
    a. Spell out every number that begins a sentence;
    b. Use numerals for every percentage and decimal number; and
    c. Use numeral for every number within a set of amounts.

11. **Numbering your page** - use Arabic numerals to number every page in your paper, except for pages that introduce the body text, such as: (a) The copyright page; (b) The dedication pages, (c) The table of contents page. Chicago Style dubs these pages as "display" pages, and you must number these pages with lowercase Roman numerals. Do not put a number on the title page, but you MUST count the title page as part of the "display" pages. The next page is left blank unless you use a copyright page. You do not number the copyright (or blank page) either. Number the next page (after the copyright or blank page) "iii" in Roman numerals, centered at the bottom of the page. When you begin the main (body) text, change from Roman numeral to Arabic numbers. Put the number "1" in the upper - right corner of the page. If you page has a chapter heading or a main heading, you can center the Arabic numeral at the bottom of the page. Number all blank pages, including any other pages. You page number must run consecutively. Position all page numbers about three - quarter of an inch from the side of the paper.

12. **Paper type** - Use standard 20 - pound regular - white bond paper that is 8.5 by 11 inches.

13. **Spacing** - Double - space between sentences and paragraphs for your entire paper's body text. However, you can single - space block captions, endnotes, footnotes, headings, and quotations.

14. **Title** - Center all text on the title page, using both horizontal and vertical alignment Uppercase all text and double - space too.

Citation Style Guide

Reference is an important of research paper. It must be consistent and easy to read across different papers. There are predefined styles stating how to set them - out - these are called citation styles. Different subjects prefer to use different subjects prefer to use different styles. Referencing is a method used to demonstrate to the readers that you have conducted a thorough and appropriate literature search and reading.

A. **APA (American Psychological Association)** - APA is an author / date - based style. This means emphasis is placed is placed on the author and the date of a piece of work to uniquely identify it.

In - text Citations

The University of Waikato released handout on how use APA reference format.

Direct quotation - use quotation marks around the quote and include page number.

Samovar and Porter (1997) point out that "Language involves attaching meaning to symbols" (p.188). Alternatively, "Language involves attaching meaning to symbols" (Samovar & Porter, 1997, p. 188)

Indirect quotation / paraphrasing - no quotation marks

Attaching meaning to symbols is considered to be the origin of written language (Samovar & Porter, 1997).

Citations from a secondary source

As hall (1977) asserts, "culture also defines boundaries of different groups" (as cited in Samovar & Porter, 1997, p. 14)

APA Examples of References Type	
In a reference list	**In - text citation**
1. **Book with one author** King, M. (2000). *Wrestling with the angel: A life of Janet Frame.* Auckland, New Zealand: Viking.	(King, 2000) or King (2000) compares Frame ....
2. **Book with two authors** Dancey, C. P., & Reidy, J (2004*). Statistics without maths for psychology: Using SPSS for Windows (3rd ed.)* Harlow, England: Paearson / Prentice Hall.	(Dancey & Reidy, 2004) or Dancey and Reidy (2004) said....
3. **Book with three to five authors** Krause, K. L. , Bochner, S & Duchesne , S. (2006). *Educational psychology for learning and teaching (2nd ed).* South Melbourne, Vic., Australia: Thompson.	(Krause, Bochner, & Duchesne, 2006)

	If used first time then in subsequent citation, (Krause et al., 2006)
4. Book or report by a corporate author e.g. organization association, government department. University of Waikato. (1967). *First hall of residence (Information series No. 3)*. Hamilton, New Zealand Author.	(University of Waikato, 1967)
5. Book chapter in edited book Helber, L E. (1995). Redeveloping mature resort for new markets. In M. V Conlin & T. Baum (Eds.), *Island tourism: Management principles and practice (pp. 105 - 113)*. Chichester, England: John Wiley	(Helber, 1995) or Helber (1995) compares luxury resort....
6. Conference paper online Bochner, S. (1996, November). *Mentoring in higher education: Issues to be addressed in developing a mentoring program*. Paper presented at the Australian Association of Research in Education Conference, Singapore. Retrieved from http://www.aare.edu.au?96pap/boch96018.txt	Bochner, 1996) or According to Bochner (1996)...
7. Course handout/lecture notes Salter, G (2007). *Lecture 3:SPLS205-07 A [PowerPoint slides]*. Hamiliton, New Zealand: University of Waikato.	(Salter, 2007)
8. Film (see Library APA referencing webpage for music and other media) Zhang, Y. (Producer/Director). (2000). *Not one less [Motion picture]*. China: Columbia Pictures.	(Zhang, 2000)
9. Journal article - academic/scholarly (electronic version) with DOI Hohepa, M., Schofield, G., & Kolt, G. S. (2006). Physical Activiity: What do high school student think? *Journal of Adolescent Health,39 (30, 326. Doi: 10.1016/j* jadohealth.2005,12.024	
10. Journal article - academic./scholarly (electronic version) with no DOI. Harrison, B., & Papa, R (2005). The development of an indigenous knowledge program in a New Zealand Maori - Language immersion school. Anthropology and Education Quarterly, 36 (1), 57 -72. Retrieved from ProQuest Education Journal database.	(Harrison & Papa, 2005) or Harrison and Papa (2005) recommend...

11. Journal article - academic / scholarly (print version) Gibbs, M (2005). The right to development and indigenous peoples: Lessons from New Zealand. World Development. 33(8), 1365-1378.	(Gibbs, 2005) or Gibbs (2005) contradicts...
12. Journal Article - academically / scholarly (Internet only - no print version) Snell, D. & Hodgetts, D. (n.d). The psychology of heavy metal communities and white supremacy. Te kura kate Aronui, 1. Retrieved from http://www.waikato.ac.nz?wfasss/tkka	(Snell & Hodgetts, n.d) or Snell and Hodgetts (n.d) suggest"..." (para.3)
13. Magazine article - popular/trade/general interest Goodwin, D. K, (2002, February 4). How I caused that story. Time, 159 (5), 69.	(Goodwin, 2002) or Goodwin (2002) defends....
14. Newspaper article - (Print version) Hartevelt, J. (2007, December 20). Boy racers. The Press, p. 3.	(Hartevelt, 2007)
15. Newspaper article (Database like Newztext Plus) (also see Library referencing webpage for Internet version) Cumming, G. (2003, April 5). Cough that shook the world. The New Zealand Herald. Retrieved from Newztext Plus database.	(Cumming, 2003)
16. Newspaper article with no author Report casts shadow on biofuel crops. (2007, October 16). Waikato, p. 21.	('Report Casts Shadow,"2007)
17. Personal Communication (Letter, telephone conversations, emails, interviews)	(H. Clarke, personal communication, March 19,2004)
18. Thesis - Institutional or personal webpage - outside the US Dewstow, R. A (2006). Using the internet to enhance teaching at the University of Waikato (Master's thesis, University of Waikato, Hamilton, New Zealand). Retrieved from http:/researchcommons.waikato.ac.nz/handle/10289/2241	(Dewstow, 2006) or Dewstow *(2006) identified...

B. **MLA (Modern Language Association)** - MLA is most often applied by the arts and humanities, particularly in the USA. It is arguably the best used of all the citation styles. The MLA system uses in - text citations rather than footnotes or endnotes. The citations in text are very brief, usually just the author's family name and relevant page number. These citations correspond to the full references in the list of works cited at the end of the document (Monash University)

In - text Citations

1. If the author's name is mentioned in the sentence, only cite the page number.
2. If the author's name is not mentioned in the sentence, cite both the name and the page number.
3. Font and capitalization must match that in the reference list.
4. Long quotations must match that in the reference list.
5. If you are citing more than one reference at the same point in a document, separate the references with a semicolon (Example: Faltado 1110; Pogoy 101).
6. If you are citing two works by the same author, put a comma after the author's name and add title words. (Boholano, "Fractality" 23) to distinguish between them in the in - text citation. Do this when citing each of the sources throughout the piece of writing.
7. If two authors have the same surname, use their first initial (H. Boholano 65).

List of Works Cited

1. The recommended heading for the reference list is work cited, which should be centered.
2. Each reference should be formatted with double - spacing and a hanging indent.
3. Capitalize the first word of the title or subtitle, and all other significant words.
4. Author's names should be listed with full forenames if known.
5. The name of the first author is inverted to list the family name first. If there are additional authors their names are not inverted.
6. If you cite more than one work by the same author, give the names in the first entry only. Thereafter, use three hyphens instead of the name.
7. If a reference does not have an author, list it by title, ignore the leading article (A, The etc.) when inserting the reference into the alphabetical cited list.
8. If you cannot validate a reference's authorship, date of publication or its authoritative instead.
9. For a journal article in an online database (e.g via the library website) include the name of the database (italicized), the medium of publication (web) and the date of access.
10. When the title page list two or more publishers which are not just more offices of the same publisher, include all of them, in the order as part of the publication information, putting a semicolon after the name of each publisher but the last.

C. **Chicago and Turabian** - These are two separate styles but are very similar, just like APA. These are widely used for history and economics. Most of the education research and social science research used APA referencing. APA requires that information be cited in 2 different ways - within the text and in a reference list at the end of the paper. The reference list should be on a new page, double spaced, and use the hanging indent method (all lines after the first one is indented). According to Chicago manual of style online, it presents two documentation systems: (1) Notes and bibliography and (2) author - date. Choosing between the two often depends on subject matter and the nature of sources cited, as each system is favored by different groups of scholars. The notes and bibliography and the arts. This style presents bibliographic information in notes, often, a bibliography. It accommodates a variety of sources, including esoteric ones less appropriate to the author - date system.

Chicago Style Examples of References Type	
In a reference list	**In - text citation**
Book: single author Michael Pollan, *The Omnivore's Dilemma: A Natural History of Four Meals* (New York: Penguin, 2006), 99 -100. Pollan, Michael. *The Omnivore's Dilemma: A Natural History of Four Meals.* New York: Peguin, 2006.	Pollan, *Omnivore's Dilemma*, 3.
Book: Two or more authors Geoffrey C. Ward and Ken Burns, *The War: An Intimate History, 1994 -1995* (New York: Knoof, 2007), 52. Ward, Geoffrey C., and Ken Burns. *The War: An Intimate History, 1941 -1945.* New York: Knopf, 2007.	Ward and Burns, *War*, 59 -61.
Book: Four or more authors, list all of the authors in the bibliography, in the note, list only the first author, followed by et al ("and other')	Barnes et al., *Plastics...*
Book published electronically Jane Austen, *Pride and Prejudice* (New York: Penguin Classics, 2007), Kindle Edition.	Austen, *Pride and Prejudice.*
Journal Article in a print journal. Joshua I. Weinstein, "*The Market in Plato's Republic,*" *Classical Philology 104 (2009): 440.*	Weinstein "*Plato's Republic,*" 452 -53.
Article in an online journal Gueorgi Kossinets and Duncan J. Watts, "Origins of Homophily in an Evolving Social Network," *American Journal of Sociology* 115 (2009): 411, assessed February 28, 2010, doi: 10.1086/599247.	Kossinets and Watts, "*Origin of Homolophily,*" 439.
Book review David Kamp, "Deconstructing Dinner," review of The Omnivore's Dillema: A Natural History of Four Meals, by Michael Pollan, New York Times, April 23, 2006, Sunday Book review, http://www.nytimes.com/2006/04/23/book/review/23kamp.	Kamp, "*Deconstructing Dinner,*"
Thesis or dissertation Mihwa Choi, "Contesting Imaginaries in Death Rituals during the Northern Song Dynasty (PhD diss., University of Chicago, 2008).	Choi,

Paper presented at a meeting or conference	
Rachel Adelman, "Such Stuff as Dreams Are Made On: God's Footstool in the Aramaic Tangumim and Midrashic Tradition" (paper presented at the annual meeting for the Society of Biblical Literature, New Orleans, Lousiana, November 21 -24,2009).	Adelam, "Such Stuff as Dreams."

Plagiarism

Plagiarism is an issue of great concern amongst the academicians. Plagiarism is a moral, ethical, and legal issue. Plagiarism has been around for centuries, but the Internet and the subsequent proliferation of information have made the problem more serious. Plagiarism is taking someone else's work and passing it off as one's own. Many people think of plagiarism as copying another's work or borrowing someone else's original ideas. But terms like "copying" and "borrowing" can disguise the seriousness of the offense. Plagiarism define as follows:

1. To steal and pass off (the ideas or words of another) as one's own
2. To use (another's production) without crediting the source.
3. To commit literary theft
4. To present as new and original an idea or product derived from an existing source.
5. In other words, plagiarism is an act of fraud. It involves both stealing someone else's work and lying about it afterward.

Types of Plagiarism

Plagiarism includes copying words or ideas from someone else without giving credit; failing to put a quotation in quotation marks; giving incorrect information about the source of a quotation; changing words but copying the sentence structure of a source without giving credit; copying so many words or ideas from a source that it makes up the majority of your work . The types of Plagiarism can be categorized and listed as given below:

1. **Sources Not Cited**

    a) **The Ghost Writer.** The writer turns in another's work, word-for-word, as his or her own.
    b) **The Photocopy.** The writer copies significant portions of text straight from a single source, without alteration.
    c) **The Potluck Paper.** The writer tries to disguise plagiarism by copying from several different sources, tweaking the sentences to make them fit together while etaining most of the original phrasing.

d) **The Poor Disguise.** Although the writer has retained the essential content of the source, he or she has altered the paper's appearance slightly by changing key words and phrases.

e) **The Labor of Laziness.** The writer takes the time to paraphrase most of the paper from other sources and make it all fit together, instead of spending the same effort on original work.

f) **The Self-Stealer.** The writer "borrows" generously from his or her previous work, violating policies concerning the expectation of originality adopted by most academic institutions.

2. **Sources Cited (But Still Plagiarized)**

a) **The Forgotten Footnote.** The writer mentions an author's name for a source but neglects to include specific information on the location of the material referenced. This often masks other forms of plagiarism by obscuring source locations.

b) **Misinformed.** The writer provides inaccurate information regarding the sources, making it impossible to find them.

c) **The Too-Perfect Paraphrase.** The writer properly cites a source but neglects to put in quotation marks text that has been copied word-for-word, or close to it. Although attributing the basic ideas to the source, the writer is falsely claiming original presentation and interpretation of the information.

d) **The Resourceful Citer.** The writer properly cites all sources, paraphrasing and using quotations appropriately. The paper contains almost no original work! It is sometimes difficult to spot this form of plagiarism because it looks like any other well-researched document.

e) **The Perfect Crime.** Well, we all know it does not exist. In this case, the writer properly quotes and cites sources in some places but goes on to paraphrase other arguments from those sources without citation. This way, the writer tries to pass off the paraphrased material as his or her own analysis of the cited material.

3. **Other types of plagiarism**

Other types of plagiarism have also been recognized. These are:

a) **Copy and Paste Plagiarism**. Any time a sentence or significant phrase intact from a source is lifted , you must use quotation marks and reference the source.

b) **Word Switch Plagiarism**. If you take a sentence from a source and change around a few words, it is still plagiarism. If you want to quote a sentence, then you need to put it in quotation marks and cite the author and article. But quoting Source articles should only be done if what the quote says is particularly useful in the point you are trying to make in what you are writing. In many cases, a quotation would not really be useful. The person who plagiarizes is sometimes just too lazy to synthesize the ideas expressed in the Source article.

c) **Metaphor Plagiarism.** Metaphors are used either to make an idea clearer or give the reader an analogy that touches the senses or emotions better than a plain description of the object or process. Metaphors, then, are an important part of an author's creative style. If you cannot come up with your own metaphor to illustrate an important idea, then use the metaphor in the Source Article, but give the author credit for it.

d) **Idea Plagiarism**. If the author of the source article expresses a creative idea or suggests a solution to a problem, the idea or solution must be clearly attributed to the author.

e) **Reasoning Style/Organization Plagiarism**. When you follow a Source Article sentence-by sentence or paragraph-by-paragraph, it is plagiarism, even though none of your sentences are exactly like those in the Source article or even in the same order. What you are copying in this case is the author's reasoning style.

Anti-Plagiarism Tools

1. **CopyCatch Gold (http://www.copycatch.freeserve.co.uk/).** A forensic linguist at CFL Software Development with extensive experience in plagiarism developed this software for teachers and students.

2. **EduTie.com (http://www.edutie.com/).** EduTie.com was founded in August 2000, and is designed to help institutions prevent Internet plagiarism. It is built on the PlagiServe (http:// www.plagiserve.com) core design. Papers submitted are compared to more than 1 billion "high risk" Web pages in an attempt to detect plagiarism. Free trials of the software are available.

3. **EVE2: Essay Verification Engine (http://www.canexus.com/eve/index.shtml).** EVE2 claims to come as close as possible to searching every site on the Internet to detect plagiarism by "employing the most advanced searching tools available to locate suspected sites.

4. **Glatt Plagiarism Program (http://www.plagiarism.com).** Dr. Barbara Glatt has developed the 3 different software programs designed to detect and prevent plagiarism. The 3 parts are the Plagiarism Teaching Program, the Plagiarism Screening Program, and the Plagiarism Self-Detection Program. A

list of publications that have reviewed the Glatt Plagiarism Program can be found. at http:// www.plagiarism.com/publications.htm.

5. **Google (http://www.google.com).** Google is not designed to be a plagiarism detection tool, but its advanced search engine capabilities are conducive to locating key phrases that may appear in students' research papers. The Google Directory also has numerous links to information about plagiarism detection devices at http:// directory.google.com/Top/Reference/Education/ Educators/Plagiarism/Detection/.

6. **Joint Information Systems Committee (JISC): (Electronic Plagiarism Detection http:// www.jisc.ac.uk/plagiarism/).** JISC completed a plagiarism project in 2001, and they are establishing a plagiarism advisory service as a result of this experience. There were 4 parts to their plagiarism project, and they include:
   a) Technical review of free-text plagiarism detection software.
   b) Technical review of source code plagiarism detection software.
   c) A pilot of free-text detection software
   d) A good practice guide to plagiarism detection.

A listserv has also been established to continue discussions dealing with academic dishonest and plagiarism issues. A copy of JISC's Technical Review of Plagiarism Detection Software Report can be accessed at http:/ /www.jisc.ac.uk/pub01/luton.pdf.

7. **JISC Plagiarism Advisory Service (http://online.northumbria.ac.uk/faculties/a rt/informationstudies/Imri/JISCPAS/site/default.htm).** JISC Plagiarism Advisory Service is a new offering that began in September 2002. It is based in the Information Management Research Institute at Northumbria University (UK). New materials are constantly being added to this plagiarism portal, but it currently offers advice & guidance, educational materials for students and other online resources. A plagiarism detection service, supported by the Joint Information Systems Committee (JISC) until August 2004, is based on the turnitin.com platform and allows instructors to conduct electronic comparisons of work complete by students.

8. **Jplag (http://www.jplag.de/).** Guido Malpohl initially developed this software which is designed to detect academic dishonesty. The software does more than merely compare the text of documents. JPlag also looks at program language syntax and program structure so it can also be used to detect stolen software parts. Instructors may use JPlag for free, but they must first set up an account in order to prevent unauthorized use by students.

9. **Library Electronic Databases (http://gateway.library.uiuc.edu/ersearch/).** The Library at the University of Illinois at UrbanaChampaign provides access to numerous

electronic resources for students and faculty. Instructors may want to consult these resources when checking for plagiarism. Full text databases like EBSCO and Expanded Academic ASAP (InfoTrac) are two obvious starting points when checking undergraduate assignments. One thing to keep in mind is that some resources that are not full text but provide abstract information are often used by students.

10. **MOSS (http://www.cs.berkeley.edu/~aiken/moss.html).** Moss or Measure of Software Similarity is a tool that has been used primarily to detect plagiarism. The way it works is that it detects similarities of C, C++, Java, Pascal, Ada, ML, Lisp or Scheme programs. Moss is free to use for instructors and staff of programming language courses only.

11. **Plagiarism.org (http://www.plagiarism.org).** University of California Berkeley students and alumni created plagiarism.org to be used to detect plagiarism. One thing to watch out for is that the software doesn't differentiate between quoted materials and original writing.

12. **The Plagiarism Resource Site (http://www.plagiarism.phys.virginia.edu/).** Lou Bloomfield, Professor of Physics at the University of Virginia, is the sole author of The Plagiarism Resource Site. The goal of this site is to "help reduce the impact of plagiarism on education and educational institutions". Numerous links are provided to sources on how to deal with plagiarism.

13. **PlagiServe (http://www.plagiserve.com/).** Olexiy Shevchenko, Max Litvin and Sasha Lugovskyy, the PlagiServe Team, came up with the concept of a plagiarism detection device in June 2000. The software used by PlagiServe not only detects papers that have been obtained from a term paper company and turned into an Instructor, but it also looks for any changes or modifications made to these papers. PlagiServe has a database of over 150,000 student essays, term papers and cliff notes, and they also send out Web robots to check "high risk" sites like Britannica.com, Refdesk.com and Encyclopedia.com for copied materials. NOTE: Instructors may want to be careful about using this particular detection device. Some indicate it may also sell term papers to students.

14. **Turnitin (http://www.turnitin.com/).** Turnitin, a plagiarism.org partner, considers themselves to be "the world's most widely recognized and trusted resource to prevent Internet plagiarism". Free trials are also available, and subscription costs vary depending on the type of plan chosen. Turnitin is currently the subject of a copyright controversy. For more information, check out the following article, "A Plagiarism Detection Tool Creates Legal Quandary" at http://chronicle.com/ free/v48/i36/36a03701.htm.

15. **WordCHECK (http://www.wordchecksystems.com/)** WordCHECK is used by a diverse group including information researchers, copyright attorneys and classroom teachers. This plagiarism detection device was developed by

Information Analytics, a Lincoln, NE company owned by Kenneth Livingston and Mark Dahmke. WordCHECK may be purchased for a fee.

Assessment Tasks

I. **Direction:** Select the correct answer below each question.

1. The words, ideas, arguments, and/or overall organization of a work are protected intellectual property,
   a) unless the work appears on the Internet.
   b) unless the copyright has run out on the work.
   c) unless it is a work of fiction.
   d) but may still be cited according to "fair use" restrictions.

2. When is it necessary to cite a source?
   a) When your ideas build on someone else's.
   b) When you are paraphrasing someone else's ideas.
   c) If you are unsure whether you should cite the source.
   d) All of the above.

3. In addition to citing sources for written texts, it is also important to reference.
   a) any information taken from standard reference works such as encyclopedias, dictionaries, or statistical sources.
   b) ideas taken from a lecture by a professor.
   c) information taken off the internet.
   d) ideas gleaned from classroom discussion.

4. Turnitin.com is used in The Human Situation for the purposes of
   a) automatic grading of papers.
   b) tracking your cumulative grades throughout the semester.
   c) detecting plagiarism in all papers.
   d) b and c

5. Two students work together on their papers. When they submit them to Turnitin.com, they turn up a 35% match. Their professors will find that.
   a) they are not guilty of plagiarism, since the ideas were derived in common.
   b) only the student to submit his paper last is guilty of plagiarism.
   c) regardless of intent, the students have committed plagiarism.
   d) the students have committed plagiarism if evidence of the intent to plagiarize can be established.

6. Identify the correct APA in-text citation for this quote from Nutrition and Mental Health by Ruth Leyse-Wallace, 2013.
   a) "Levels and ratios of essential fatty acids appear to be linked to anger, violence, hostility, and aggressive behavior."

b) Leyse-Wallace (2013) notes that "levels and ratios of essential fatty acids appear to be linked to anger, violence, hostility, and aggressive behavior" (p. 31).
c) Leyse-Wallace notes that "levels and ratios of essential fatty acids appear to be linked to anger, violence, hostility, and aggressive behavior" (2013, p. 31).
d) Leyse-Wallace (2013) notes that "levels and ratios of essential fatty acids appear to be linked to anger, violence, hostility, and aggressive behavior."

7. Identify the correct APA in-text citation for the following summary from this source: "Multituberculates of the Lac Pelletier Lower Fauna, Late Eocene (Duchesnean), of Saskatchewan" by John E. Storer, 1993, Canadian Journal of Earth Sciences, v. 30, iss. 8, pages 1613-1617.
a) Two species of multituberculate mammals were present in Saskatchewan in the Late Eocene (1993).
b) Two species of multituberculate mammals were present in Saskatchewan in the Late Eocene (Storer, p. 1617).
c) Two species of multituberculate mammals were present in Saskatchewan in the Late Eocene (Storer, 1993).
d) Two species of multituberculate mammals were present in Saskatchewan in the Late Eocene.

8. Identify the correct APA in-text citation for this source with no author: Thanks a lot, bro. (2016, August 8). Maclean's, 129(31), 9.
a) (n.a., 2016)
b) (Maclean's, 2016, p. 9)
c) (unknown, 2016, p. 9)
d) (Thanks a lot, 2016, p. 9)

9. Identify the correct APA reference format for this book: Jellyfish: A Natural History by Lisa-Ann Gershwin, 2016, University of Chicago Press, Chicago.
a) Gershwin, L. (2016). Jellyfish: A natural history. The University of Chicago Press.
b) Gershwin, Lisa-Ann. (2016). Jellyfish: A natural history. Chicago: The University of Chicago Press.
c) Gershwin, Lisa-Ann. Jellyfish: A natural history. Chicago: The University of Chicago Press, 2016.
d) Gershwin, L. 2016. Jellyfish: A natural history. The University of Chicago Press.

10. Identify the correct APA reference format for this journal article: "Visualization of a lost painting by Vincent van Gogh using synchrotron radiation based X-ray fluorescence elemental mapping" by J. Dik, K. Janssens, G. Van der Snickt, L. van der Loeff, K. Rickers, & M. Cotte in

Analytical Chemistry, 2008, v. 80, iss. 16, pages 6436-6442. https://pubs.acs.org/doi/10.1021/ac800965g

   a) Dik, J. et al. (2008). Visualization of a lost painting by Vincent van Gogh using synchrotron radiation based X-ray fluorescence elemental mapping. Analytical Chemistry, 80(16), 6436-6442. https://pubs.acs.org/doi/10.1021/ac800965g

   b) Dik, J., Janssens, K., Van der Snickt, G., van der Loeff, L., Rickers, K., & Cotte, M. (2008). Visualization of a lost painting by Vincent van Gogh using synchrotron radiation based X-ray fluorescence elemental mapping. Analytical Chemistry, 80(16), 6436-6442. https://pubs.acs.org/doi/10.1021/ac800965g

   c) Dik, J., Janssens, K., Van der Snickt, G., van der Loeff, L., Rickers, K., & Cotte, M. (2008). Visualization of a lost painting by vincent van gogh using synchrotron radiation based X-ray fluorescence elemental mapping. Analytical Chemistry, 80.

   d) Dik, J., Janssens, K., Van der Snickt, G., van der Loeff, L., Rickers, K., & Cotte, M. (2008). "Visualization of a lost painting by vincent van gogh using synchrotron radiation based X-ray fluorescence elemental mapping." Analytical Chemistry, 80(16), 6436-6442. Web. 30 Aug. 2016.

II. **Direction:** Make a Literature Review on the following thesis statement using the Literature review strategies.

1. With more and more teens using smartphones and social media, cyber bullying is on the rise. Cyber bullying puts a lot of stress on many teens, and can cause depression, anxiety, and even suicidal thoughts. Parents should limit the usage of smart phones, monitor their children's online activity, and report any cyber bullying to school officials in order to combat this problem.

2. Corporations should provide more work from home opportunities and six-hour workdays so that office workers have a better work-life balance and are more likely to be productive when they are in the office.

3. With more information readily available than ever before, it is crucial that students are prepared to examine the material they're reading and determine whether or not it's a good source or if it has misleading information. Teaching student's digital literacy and helping them to understand the difference between opinion or propaganda from legitimate, real information is integral.

4. A degree from a university provides invaluable lessons on life and a future career, but not every high school student should be encouraged to attend a university directly after graduation. Some students may benefit from a trade school or a "gap year" where they can think more

intensely about what it is they want to do for a career and how they can accomplish.

Performance Tasks.

Design and Make a Literature Review

1. From your approved research title and statement of the problem write a literature review. The structure of your literature review should have the following:
    a) A synopsis of the subject, problem, or theory under contemplation, along with the purposes of the literature review.
    b) Dissection of works under review into theme or categories (e.g., activities that support a particular position, those that propose an entirely new way).
    c) An explanation of how each work is alike to and differs from the others.
    d) Conclusion as to which parts are best considered in the argument of the pertinent area of research.
2. Submit a five – to ten pages literature review. It must have an introduction, a body, a conclusion as well as citations.

Rubric for Writing the Literature Review

Criteria	Excellent 16-20	Very Good 11-15	Good 6-10	Need Improvement 1-5
Organization	The structure is intuitive and sufficiently inclusive of important constructs and variables of the proposed study.	A workable structure has been presented for presenting relevant literature related to the constructs and variables of the proposed study.	The structure of the literature is review is weak; it does not identify important ideas, constructs or variables related to the research purpose, questions, or context.	The structure of the literature review is incomprehensible, irrelevant, or confusing.
Literature Review	The narrative integrates critical and logical details from the peer- viewed theoretical and research literature. Each key construct and variable is grounded in the literature.	Key constructs and variables are connected with relevant, reliable theoretical and research literature.	A key construct or variable is not connected with the research literature, selected literature is from unreliable sources. Literary supports are vague or ambiguous.	The review of literature is missing; it consists of nonresearched based articles. Prepositions are irrelevant, inaccurate, or inappropriate.

Mechanics	There are no errors in punctuation, and spelling	There are almost no errors in punctuation, capitalization, and spelling.	There are many errors in punctuation, capitalization, and spelling.	There are numerous and distracting errors in punctuation, capitalization, and spelling.
Citations	All works are cited done in the correct format with no errors	Some works are cited in the correct format. Inconsistent are evident	Few works are cited but done in the correct format.	No sources are cited in the review.

CHAPTER IV:

UNDERSTANDING WAYS TO COLLECT DATA

<table>
<tr><td>

LEARNING OBJECTIVES

At the end of this chapter, students should be able to:
1. describes adequately research design (either quantitative or qualitative), sample, instrument used in quantitative research, data collection and analysis procedures.
2. Presents written research methodology.

</td></tr>
</table>

Research Methodology, Design and Methods

Once you are well into your literature review, it is time to start thinking about the study you will design to answer the gap you identified. Which methodology will you use to gather the data for your research? Will you use a qualitative, quantitative, or mixed methods methodology? You will choose a research method that best aligns with your research question.

To evaluate which type of methodology will be most appropriate, you will work closely with your research adviser or teacher. However, as you are reading the literature, take a look at past studies that focus on your topic, or a similar topic. What kind of research methodology do you see being used most often? Once you have an idea about the general methodology type that would suit your research, consult with your research adviser on the possibility of using that methodology. Finding a research design strategy is similar to the research process as a whole: first, locate general information on research design and methodologies, then gain background knowledge on the methodology you feel would most appropriately address the type of data you will be collecting, and finally choose a methodology and test/measurement to use in your research.

Research Paradigms, also known as worldviews, are the long-standing philosophical assumptions, principles, and tenets that guide particular and sometimes prescriptive protocol for systematic research that may differ by discipline. Examples include positivism/post-positivism, interpretivism/constructivism, critical theory, and pragmatism.

Research Methodology is the system of methods commonly referred to as quantitative, qualitative, or mixed methods.

Research Design refers to the assembly of choices for the techniques to be employed within a respective study that may include the research approach or paradigmatic tradition such as a quasi-experimental design in quantitative research or phenomenology in qualitative research.

Research Methods are the systematic tools used to recruit, sample, collect, analyze, and/or interpret information. Think of methods as the tools and techniques used for data collection and analysis. There are more methods than listed in the illustration.

The following techniques outline how to locate information about research methodology from reference books, scholarly articles, and theses.

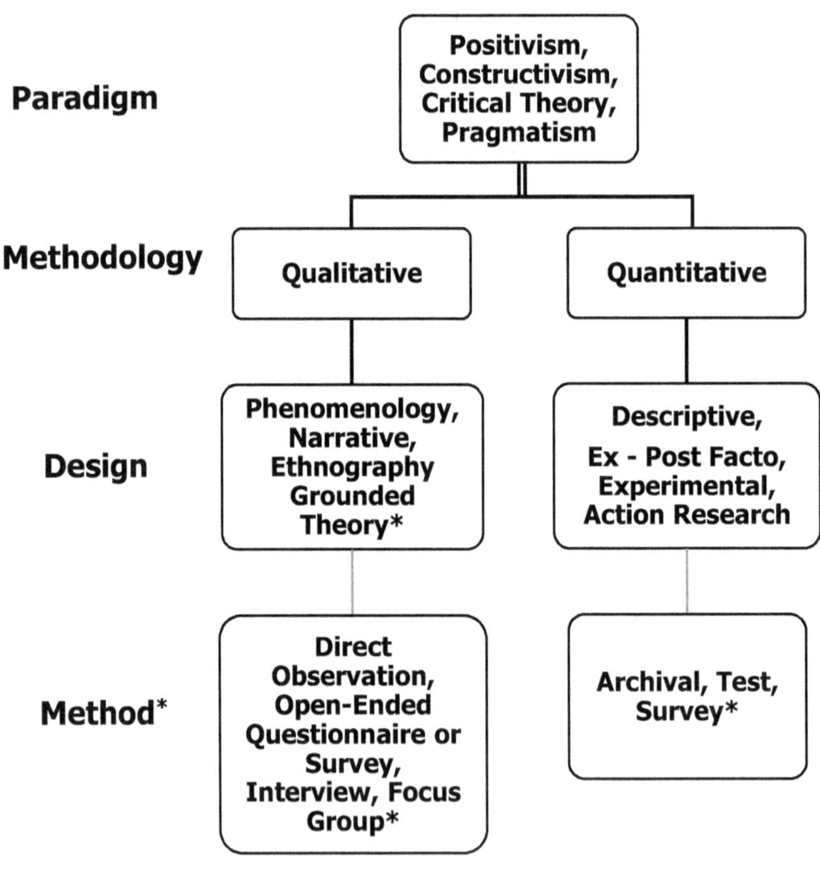

Not an exhaustive list

Research Methodology

Research methodology simply refers to the practical "how" of any given piece of research. More specifically, it is about how a researcher systematically designs a study to ensure valid and reliable results that address the research aims and objectives. For example, how did the researcher go about deciding:

1. What data to collect (and what data to ignore)

2. Who to collect it from (in research, this is called "sampling design")

3. How to collect it (this is called "data collection methods")

4. How to analyze it (this is called "data analysis methods")

In research you will find a research methodology chapter which covers the aspects mentioned above. Importantly, a good methodology chapter in research explains not just what methodological choices were made, but also explains why they were made.

In other words, the methodology should justify the design choices, by showing that the chosen methods and techniques are the best fit for the research aims and objectives and will provide valid and reliable results. A good research methodology provides scientifically sound findings, whereas a poor methodology does not.

According to Creswell (2003) the decision of what method a researcher employs depends on

1. the research problem
2. the researcher's experience,
3. the reporting audience,
4. whether the researcher wants to specify the kind of information to be collected or let it arise from the data being collected, and
5. whether data to be collected is numeric or text.

Types of Research Methodologies

1. **Qualitative.** A methodology for exploring and understanding the meaning individuals or groups ascribe to a social or human problem. The question and procedures are emerging. It characterized by inductive analysis and flexibility.
2. **Quantitative.** A methodology for testing objective theories by examining the relationship among variables. Variables can be measured, typically on instruments, and numbered data can be analyzed using statistical procedures. Characterized by a structure and deductive data analysis. It aims at generalizability.
3. **Mixed research** combines quantitative and qualitative approaches by including both quantitative and qualitative data in a single study.

Emphases of Quantitative, Qualitative and Mixed Research (Sage, 2020)

Criteria	Quantitative	Qualitative	Mixed
Scientific Method	Confirmatory or "top-down" the researcher test hypotheses and theory with data.	Exploratory or "bottom-up" the researcher generates or constructs knowledge, hypotheses, and grounded theory from data collected during fieldwork.	Confirmatory and exploratory
Ontology (nature of reality/truth)	Objective, material, structural, agreed -upon.	Subjective, mental, personal, and constructed.	Pluralism; appreciation of objective, subjective, and intersubjective realities and their interrelations.
Epistemology	Scientific realism; search for truth; justification by empirical confirmation of hypotheses; universal scientific standards.	Relativism; individual and group justification; varying standards.	Dialectical pluralism; pragmatic justification (what works for whom in specific contexts); mixture of universal (always be ethical) and community – specific needs – based standards.
View of human thought and behavior	Regular and predictable	Situational, social, contextual, personal, and unpredictable.	Dynamic, complex, and partially predictable – multiple influences include environment / nurture, biology/ nature, free will/ agency, and chance/ fortuity.
Most common research objective	Quantitative / numerical description, causal explanation, and prediction.	Qualitative/subjective description, empathetic understanding, and explanation.	Multiple objectives; provide complex and fuller explanation and understanding; understand multiple perspectives.
Interest	Identify general scientific laws; inform national policy	Understand and appreciate particular groups and individuals; inform local policy	Connect theory and practice; understand multiple causation, nomothetic (general), causation, and idiographic (local, particular, individual), causation; connect national and local interests and policy.
Focus	Narrow – angle lens, testing specific hypotheses.	Multilens focus	Wide – angle and "deep – angle" lens, examining the breadth and depth of phenomena to learn more about them.
Nature of observation	Study behavior under controlled conditions; isolate the causal effects of single variables.	Study group and individuals in natural settings; attempt to understand insider' views, meanings, and perspectives.	Study multiple contexts, perspectives, or conditions; study multiple factors as they operate together.
Form of data collected	Collect quantitative data based on precise measurement using structured and validated data-collection instruments	collect qualitative data such as in-depth interviews, participant observations, field notes, and open-ended	Collect multiple kinds of data.

		questions. The researcher is the primary data -collection instrument.	
Nature of data	Variables	Words, images, categories	Mixture of variables, words, categories, and images
Data analysis	Identify statistical relationship variables.	Use descriptive data; search for local patterns, themes and holistic features; and appreciate and articulate difference/ variation.	Quantitative and Qualitative analysis used separately and in combination.
Results	Generalize findings providing representation of objective outsider viewpoint of populations.	Particularistic findings; provision of insider viewpoints.	Provision of "subjective insider" and "objective outsider" viewpoint; presentation and integration of multiple dimensions and perspectives.
Form of final report	Formal statistical report (e.g., with correlations, comparison of means, and reporting of statistical significance of findings).	Less formal narrative report with rich contextual description and direct quotation from research participants	Mixture of number and narrative.

Essential Elements of Research Methodology

1. **Research design.** It is a very important aspect of research methodology which describe the research mode (whether it is qualitative, quantitative, or mixed research, or if the researcher will use a specific research type e.g., descriptive, survey, historical, case or experimental).
2. **Respondent of the study.** This describes the target population and the sample frame.
3. **Instrument of the study.** It describes the specific type of research instrument that will be used such as questionnaire, checklist, questionnaire -checklist, interview, schedule, teacher -made-tests, and the like.
4. **Establishing and validating reliability.** The instrument must pass the validity and reliability test before it is utilized.
5. **Data Analysis**. One of the many ways of establishing the objectivity of research findings is by subjecting the data to different but appropriate data analysis and processes.

Research Design

The function of a research design is to ensure that the evidence obtained enables you to effectively address the research problem as unambiguously as possible. In social sciences research, obtaining evidence relevant to the research problem generally entails specifying the type of evidence needed to test a theory, to evaluate a program, or to accurately describe a phenomenon. However, researchers can often begin their investigations far too early before they have thought critically about what information is required to answer the study's research questions. Without attending to these design issues beforehand, the conclusions drawn risk being weak and unconvincing and, consequently, will fail to adequate address the overall research problem.

Kinds of Qualitative Research Design

Qualitative research is a means for exploring and understanding the meaning individuals or groups ascribe to a social or human problem. The process of research involves emerging questions and procedures, data typically collected in the participant's setting, data analysis inductively building from particulars to general themes, and the researcher making interpretations of the meaning of the data. The final written report has a flexible structure. Those who engage in this form of inquiry support a way of looking at research that honors an inductive style, a focus on individual meaning, and the importance of rendering the complexity of a situation (adapted from Creswell, 2007).

These are the four common kinds of qualitative research design.

1. **Narrative** its collect stories from individuals (and documents, and group conversations) about individuals lived and told experiences. These stories may emerge from a story told to the researcher, a story that is co-constructed between the researcher and the participant, and a story intended as a performance to convey some message or point. Thus, there may be a strong collaborative feature of narrative research as the story emerges through the interaction or dialogue of the researcher and the participant(s).

2. **Phenomenology.** It describes the common meaning for several individuals of their lived experiences of a concept or a phenomenon. it focuses on describing what all participants have in common as they experience a phenomenon (e.g., grief is universally experienced). The basic purpose of phenomenology is to reduce individual experiences with a phenomenon to a description of the universal essence (a "grasp of the very nature of the thing.

3. **Grounded Theory.** intended is to move beyond description and to generate or discover a theory, a "unified theoretical explanation" for a process or an action. Participants in the study would all have experienced the process, and the development of the theory might help explain practice or provide a framework for further research. A key idea is that this theory development does not come "off the shelf" but rather is generated or "grounded" in data from participants who have experienced the process. Thus, grounded theory is a qualitative research design in which the inquirer

generates a general explanation (a theory) of a process, an action, or an interaction shaped by the views of a large number of participants.

4. **Ethnography**. it focuses on an entire culture sharing group. It describes and interprets the shared and learned patterns of values, behaviors, beliefs, and language of a culture-sharing group. As a process, ethnography involves extended observations of the group, most often through participant observation, in which the researcher is immersed in the day-to-day lives of the people and observes and interviews the group participants. Ethnographers study the meaning of the behavior, the language, and the interaction among members of the culture-sharing group.

Kinds of Quantitative Research Design

Quantitative research is a means for testing objective theories by examining the relationship among variables. These variables, in turn, can be measured, typically on instruments, so that numbered data can be analyzed using statistical procedures. The final written report has a set structure consisting of introduction, literature and theory, methods, results, and discussion (Creswell, 2008). Like qualitative researchers, those who engage in this form of inquiry have assumptions about testing theories deductively, building in protections against bias, controlling for alternative explanations, and being able to generalize and replicate the findings.

There are four basic types of quantitative research, these are:

1. **Descriptive Research Design** - According to Ochave (1992), the principal aim of descriptive research is to describe the nature and the time of study and to explore the causes of phenomenon. It is also purposive process of gathering, analyzing , classifying and tabulating data about prevailing conditions, practices, belief, processes, trends cause – effect relationship and then make adequate and accurate interpretation about such data with or without the aid of statistical methods. It is concerned with the most appropriate methods to use to come up with adequate interpretation of the data and is purposive for accurate utilization of the significant variables that needs to emphasize the true meaning of the gathered data.

Classification of Descriptive Research

a) **Descriptive - Correlational Research** - test for the relationship between two variables. Performing correctional research is done to establish what the effect of one on the other might be and how that affects the relationship. The purpose is to use two or more variables to better understand the condition of events that we encounter, to predict future conditions and events and correlation does not always mean causation (Almeida et. al, 2016).

b) **Descriptive - Survey Research** - this research methods are employed to measure the existing phenomenon without inquiring into why it exists. In such studies, you do not consider the relationship between the variables. Your main intention is to use your data for problem solving rather than for hypothesis testing. Survey research have two scopes: census and sample. Census is a survey that covers the entire population of interest. Sample survey, on the other hand, is more which deals only with a portion of the population (Ochave, et al., 1992).

c) **Descriptive - Status Research** - this approach to problem - solving seeks to answer question to real facts relating to existing conditions. This is a technique of quantitative description which determines the prevailing conditions in a group of cases chosen for study. Several descriptive - status research stress current conditions with the assumption that things will change. They cover many traits or characteristics of the group (Calmorin & Calmorin, 2007).

d) **Descriptive - Analysis Research** - this method of research determines or describes the nature of an object by separating it into parts. Its purpose is to discover the nature of things. The researcher should determine the composition, structure. He also determines the individual parts and units integrated into an internal system. He should consider the forces that hold them together, and the strains that tend to destroy the system apart. He analyzes what makes the system   work and regulates it (Zulueta & Costales, 2003).

e) **Descriptive - Classification Research -** this method is employed in natural sciences subjects, namely: Biology, Botany, Zoology, Phycology, Ichthyology, conchology, and like. The specimens collected, identified, and classified from taxonomic order (Calmorin & Calmorin, 2007).

f) **Descriptive - Evaluation Research** - this kind of research aims to assess the effects, impacts or outcomes of practices, policies, or program (Faltado, et al. 2016).

2. **Ex - Post Facto (Causal - Comparative) Research Design** - it looks to uncover a cause-and-effect relationship. This research is not conducted between the two groups on each other. They look solely for a statistically relationship between the two variable it tries to identify, specially, how the different groups are affected by the same circumstance. Causal - comparative research involves comparison. The study of two or more groups is done without

focusing on their relations. The use of statistical is engaged to synthesize the data.

3. **Action Research Design** - this research follows a cyclical process. First, the researcher identifies a problem and determines a plan of action to address it. Then, the action plan is implemented, and data is gathered to determine the effects of the action implemented. The information gathered during the implementation phase is analyzed and evaluated to gain a better understanding of the problem and determine the effectiveness of solution implemented. Action research is pragmatic and solution - driven, and any information gathered is used to identify and implement a solution to the problem. This design is appropriate for community - based situations. It requires the researcher to directly relate with his or her subjects and the community.

4. **Experimental Research Design** - This type of research seeks to determine the effect of one or more manipulative factors upon a dependent variable under controlled condition on a carefully controlled sample. The design compares the result obtained from an experimental sample with the control sample, which is practically identical to the experimental sample except for the one aspect whose effect is being tested. According to Ochave (1992) it also blueprints of the procedure that enables the researcher to test his hypothesis by reaching valid conclusions about relationships between independent and dependent variables and its conceptual framework within which the experiment is conducted.

   A. **Quasi - Experimental Research Design** - this type of design use to identify differences between two or more groups to explain causation. It allows researchers more control to make assumptions about causation and implication of findings. It is also useful when researchers want to study particular groups in which groups members cannot be randomly assigned. A major drawback to using quasi - experimental design is that these designs typically have less internal validity than do true experimental design. (Serrano, 2016b).

      The following are some types of quasi - experimental design.

      a) **One - group posttest - only design** - type of experimental study in which only one group receives a treatment and is then measured in a posttest after treatment. In this design, there is no available comparison group or pretest data or baseline condition to compare with. This design is best implemented as an evaluation model.

      b) **Static group comparison design** - this design attempt to make up for the lack of control groups but falls short in relation to showing if a change has occurred. In the static group comparison study, two groups are chosen, one of which receives the treatment and the other does not. A posttest score is then determined to measure the difference, after treatment, between the two groups. As you can see, this study does not include any pre - testing and therefore any difference between the two groups prior to study are unknown.

c) **Nonequivalent control group design** - In nonequivalent control group design, a treatment group and a comparison group are compared using pretest and posttest measures. However, these groups are not randomly selected because they constitute naturally assembled groups. The assignment of X (the treatment) to one group or the other is randomly selected by the researcher.

d) **Time series design** - a quasi - experimental research design in which periodic measurements are made on a defined group of individuals both before and after implementation of an intervention. Time series studies are often conducted for the purpose of determining the intervention or treatment effect.

e) **Equivalent time - samples** - this design involves periodic introduction of treatment followed by measurement with the treatments varied consistently over time.

f) **Multiple time series design** - a type of quasi - experimental design where a series of periodic measurement is taken from two groups of test units (an experimental group and a control). The experimental group is exposed to a treatment and then another series of periodic measurements is taken from both groups.

g) **Equivalent material design** - this design involves giving equivalent samples of materials to subjects imparting interventions, and then making observation.

B. **True Experimental Research Design** - The true experimental research design control for nearly all sources of internal and external validity there is one obvious characteristics of these design and this is randomization. Also, there is the presence of a control group (Ochave, 1992).

According to Garcia (2003) Internal validity in experimental research refers to the basic minimum without which any experiment cannot be interpreted. The question a researcher must answer is whether the experimental treatment did make a difference in the experiment. On the other hand, External validity is the extent to which the results of an experimental can be generalized to people and environmental conditions outside the context of the experiment. It asks the question, how generalizable is the experiment? To what population, setting, treatment variables and measurement variables can be effect as noted in the experiment be generalized?

Classification of True Experimental Research Design

a) **Pretest - Posttest Control Group Design -** In this design, the experimental and control groups are carefully selected through appropriate randomization procedures. Each group is pre - tested on the dependent variable. Then the experimental condition or treatment is administered to the experimental group not to the control group, keeping all conditions the same for both groups. This is necessary so that the only difference is the manipulation of the independent variable. Each group is then post - tested on the dependent variable.

b) **Solomon Four Group Design -** This design is an extension of the pretest - posttest control group design and is used to eliminate the effect of pretest. It involves random assignment of subjects to four groups, with two groups being pretested and the two not. One of the pretested groups and one of the unpretested groups is subjected to experimental treatment. All the four groups, however, are post tested at the end of the experiment. Data are analyzed by doing an analysis of variance of the posttest scores.

c) **Posttest - only Control Group Design-** this design is the same as the pretest - posttest control group design, except that there are no pretests of the dependent variables.

C. **Pre - Experimental Research Design** - these are designs that do not possess two or more characteristics of experimental research.

a) **One - Shot Case Study** - In this design, the researcher administers a treatment and then makes an observation.

b) **One - Group Pretest - Posttest Design** - In this design, a single group of subjects is given a pretest, then the treatment and then test.

c) **Static Group Comparison** - In these two randomly selected groups are designed by chance, one to be the experimental group, the other the control group. The experimental group is exposed to variable X; the control group is not. At the close of the experiment, both groups are post tested, and a comparison is made between posttest result of each group to determine what has been the effect of the treatment.

Kind of Mixed Research Design

Mixed methods research is an approach to inquiry that combines or associates both qualitative and quantitative forms. It involves philosophical assumptions, the use of qualitative and quantitative approaches, and the mixing of both approaches in a study. Thus, it is more than simply collecting and analyzing both kinds of data; it also involves the use of both approaches in tandem so that the overall strength of a study is greater than either qualitative or quantitative research (Creswell & Plano Clark, 2007).

There are three common Kind of mixed methods design.

1. **Explanatory Sequential Mixed Design**. It is a design in mixed methods that appeals to individuals with a strong quantitative background or from fields relatively new to qualitative approaches. It involves a two-phase project in which the researcher collects quantitative data in the first phase, analyzes the results, and then uses the results to plan (or build on to) the second, qualitative phase. The quantitative results typically inform the types of participants to be purposefully selected for the qualitative phase and the types of questions that will be asked of the participants. The overall intent of this design is to have the qualitative data help explain in more detail the initial quantitative results. A typical procedure might involve collecting survey data in the first phase, analyzing the data, and then following up with qualitative interviews to help explain the survey responses.

2. **Exploratory Sequential Mixed design**. The reverse of the explanatory sequential approach and start with a qualitative phase first followed by a quantitative phase. Exploratory sequential mixed design is design in which the researcher first begins by exploring with qualitative data and analysis and then uses the findings in a second quantitative phase. Like the explanatory sequential approach, the second database builds on the results of the initial database. The intent of the strategy is to develop better measurements with specific samples of populations and to see if data from a few individuals (in qualitative phase) can be generalized to a large sample of a population (in quantitative phase). For example, the researcher would first collect focus group data, analyze the results, develop an instrument based on the results, and then administer it to a sample of a population.

In this case, there may not be adequate instruments measuring the concepts with the sample that the investigator wishes to study. In effect, the researcher employs a three-phase procedure with the first phase as exploratory, the second as instrument development, and the third as administering the instrument to a sample of a population.

3. **Concurrent Triangulation Mixed Design**. In this design only one data collection phase is used, during which quantitative and qualitative data collection and analysis are conducted separately yet concurrently. The findings are integrated during the interpretation phase of the study. Usually, equal priority is given to both types of research.

4. **Concurrent Embedded Mixed Design**. In this design only one data collection phase is used, during which quantitative and qualitative data collection and analysis are conducted separately yet concurrently. The findings are integrated during the interpretation phase of the study. Usually, equal priority is given to both types of research.

Illustrative Example 1 of Research Methods & Design

Effectiveness of Claim, Evidence, and Reasoning as an Innovation to Develop Students' Scientific Argumentative Writing Skills (Samosa, 2020b)

Research Design

The researcher employed concurrent triangulation mixed design. According to Fraenkel and Wallen (2010), it uses both quantitative and qualitative methods to study the same phenomenon in to determine if the two converge upon a single understanding of research problem investigated. In this design quantitative and qualitative methods are given equal priority, and all data are collected simultaneously.

Illustrative Example 2 of Research Methods & Design

Cultivating Research Culture: Capacity Building Program Toward Initiatives to Improve Teachers Self-Efficacy , Research Anxiety and Research Attitude (Samosa, 2021d)

Research Methods & Design

The descriptive research design was employed since the present study attempts to assess the effectiveness of capacity building program in the teachers' level of research self-efficacy, research anxiety and research attitude among the faculty members of Graceville National High School.In addition, the researcher used descriptive-evaluation research to accomplish the purpose of the study. Samosa (2020) pointed out that descriptive-evaluation research is typically designed to determine the causes or consequences of processes, policies, practices, or programs. This investigation approach includes the collection of data to address questions related to the status of the study subject. It seeks to identify the essence of the situation as it occurs at the time of the analysis and to examine the causes of the situation.

Sampling Design and Procedures

The basic unit for a survey is the population of the area in which it is performed. It is not usually possible to include the entire population so that people are selectively chosen to participate in a survey.

Sampling is the process of choosing a representative part of the population under study. "Typical" or representative of the population" means that a part of the population is chosen in such a manner that the characteristics and variation are reflected. It is, therefore, not just taking any part but rather that which is representative of the entire population (Sanchez, 1997).

The problem of sampling is one of the most important as well as one of the most difficult problems in social and behavioral science researchers. Orth (1976), a senior research scientist, point out that good sampling is an effective means of reducing the number of persons contacted to get a relatively accurate picture of the sample population's attitude and opinion.

A sample is a limited but representative subset of a population. It must however be adequate in size in order to be reliable. A good sample must be representative of the universe or population. A sample that is not representative of the population is known as biased sample. This may be due to imperfect instruments, the personal qualities of the observer, defective technique, or other causes (Yule & Kendall, 1990).

The term "population" is not necessarily synonymous with a population of people. A statistical population or universe may consist of attributes, qualities or behavior of people, the behavior of inanimate objects such as dice or coins, cities or city block, households or dwelling structures, the day's output of a factory, or opinions of the electorate of an entire nation.

There are two groups of population: the target population and the accessible population. The target population is composed of the entire group of people or objects to which the researcher wishes to generalize the findings of the study, while the accessible population is a portion of the population to which the researcher has reasonable access. For example, in a study about common difficulties encountered by senior high school students in their first semester of school year 2017-2018, the target population may be all senior high school students in metro manila. However, the researcher may have access only to the students of a specific school - these students comprise the accessible population.

Researchers commonly select samples for study rather than entire populations due to constraints in budget, time, and manpower. A good sample should be representative of the population, such that the characteristics of the population - especially those pertinent to the study - are reflected in the sample with a fair amount of accuracy.

The individual participants in the study are often referred to as subject or respondents. The subjects are individuals or entities which serve as the focus of the study. Respondents are individuals or groups of people who actively serve as source of information during data collection. The subjects of the study may also be its respondents, but there also times that these are two groups of different individuals or entities. Subject and respondents may also be referred to as elements - particularly if said elements are objects, rather than people.

Take for example a study focused on the behavior of the students who belong to broken families. The students who belong to these families are the subjects of the study, which may also be the respondents the researcher seeks to interview directly. If the researcher interviews or surveys the classmates of these students, the students remain the subjects and the classmate then become the respondents.

A statistic is a number describing a property of a sample, whereas a parameter is a number describing a property of a population. A statistic can be used to estimate the parameter in what Is called a statistical inference. For example: a researcher, examining all marriages in the Philippines in the year 2016, wants to find a parameter - the mean age of all men in those marriages. From sample of 1,000 subjects, she obtains mean of 31 years. This figure is a statistic. Using this figure, she concludes that the mean age of Filipino men who married in 2016 is likely to be close to 31, as well.

It is important for the researcher to us an acceptable sample size to ensure that their study will be accurate. Generally, the larger the sample, the, more reliable the result of the study will be. Hence, it is advisable to have a sample large enough to yield reliable results, yet small enough to be manageable within the constraints of the study.

Advantages of Sampling

The advantages of sampling are as follows:
1. **It saves time, money, and effort.** The researcher can save time, money, and effort because the number of subjects involved is small. With

only a small number of subjects to be collected, tabulated, presented, analyzed and interpreted, the use of sample gives comprehensive information of the results of the study.

2. **It is more effective.** Sampling is more effective if every individual of the population without bias has an equal chance of being included in the sample and data are scientifically collected, analyzed, and interpreted.
3. **It is faster, cheaper and economical.** Since sample is only "drop in a bucket," the collection, tabulation, presentation, analysis and interpretation of data are rapid and less expensive due to small number of subjects and few copies of the questionnaires are used.
4. **It is more accurate.** Fewer errors are made due to small size of data involved n collection, tabulation, presentation, analysis and interpretation.
5. **It gives more comprehensive information.** Since there is a thorough investigation of the study due to small sample, the results give more comprehensive information because all members of the population have an equal chance of being included in the sample.

Disadvantage of Sampling

If sampling design has strength, it also has its weakness. The disadvantages of sampling are as follows.

1. Sample data involve more care in preparing detailed subclassification due to small to small number of subjects.
2. If the sampling plan is not correctly designed and followed, the results may be misleading.
3. Sampling requires an expert to conduct the study in an area. If this is lacking, the result can be erroneous.
4. The characteristics to be observed may occur rarely in a population, for instance over 30 years of teaching experience o teachers with outstanding performance.
5. Complicated sampling plans are laborious to prepare.

Factors to consider in determining the sample size. (Macmillian & Schumacher, 1989)

1. Homogeneity of the population.
2. Degree of precision desired by the researcher.
3. Types of sampling procedure.
4. The Types of research
5. Research hypothesis
6. Financial constraints
7. Importance of the results

8. Numbers of variables studied.
9. Methods of data collection

Various approaches to determining the Sample size.

1. Sample sizes as small as 30 are generally adequate to ensure that the sampling distribution of the mean will approximate the normal curve (Shott, 1990).
2. When the total population is equal to or less than, this same number may serve as the sample size. This called universal sampling.
3. Slovin's formula is used to compute for sample size (Sevilla, 1990).

$$n = \frac{N}{1+Ne^2}$$

Where n stand for a sample; N, the population size, and e is for desired margin of error

Example: the population total is 8,000 with a desired 2% margin of error

Given: $N = 8,000$; $e = 0.02$

$$n = \frac{N}{1+Ne^2}$$

$$= \frac{8,000}{1+8,000\,(0.02)^2}$$

$$= \frac{8,000}{1+8,000\,(0.0004)}$$

$$= \frac{8,000}{1+3.2}$$

$$= \frac{8,000}{4.2}$$

$$= 1,905$$

4. Minimum Sample Size Recommendations for Most Common Quantitative and Qualitative Research Designs by experts.

Research Design	Minimum Sample Size Suggestion
1. **Correlational**	64 participants for one-tailed hypotheses; 82 participants for two-tailed hypotheses (Onwuegbuzie et al., 2004)
2. **Causal-Comparative**	51 participants per group for one-tailed hypotheses; 64 participants for two-tailed hypotheses (Onwuegbuzie et al., 2004)
3. **Experimental**	21 participants per group for one-tailed hypotheses (Onwuegbuzie et al., 2004)
4. **Case Study**	3-5 participants (Creswell, 2002)
5. **Phenomenological**	≤ 10 interviews (Creswell, 1998);∃ ≥ 6 (Morse, 1994)
6. **Grounded Theory**	15-20 (Creswell, 2002); 20-30 (Creswell, 2007)
7. **Ethnography**	1 cultural group (Creswell, 2002); 30-50 interviews (Morse, 1994)
8. **Ethological**	100-200 units of observation (Morse, 1994)

Sampling Design	Minimum Sample Size Suggestion
1. **Subgroup Sampling Design**	≥ 3 participants per subgroup (Onwuegbuzie & Leech, 2007c)
2. **Nested Sampling Design**	≥ 3 participants per subgroup (Onwuegbuzie & Leech, 2007c)

Data Collection Procedure	Minimum Sample Size Suggestion
1. **Interview**	12 participants (Guest, Bunce, & Johnson, 2006)
2. **Focus Group**	6-9 participants (Krueger, 2000); 6-10 participants (Langford, Schoenfeld, & Izzo, 2002; Morgan, 1997); 6-12 participants (Johnson & Christensen, 2004); 6-12 participants (Bernard, 1995); 8–12 participants (Baumgartner, Strong, & Hensley, 2002). 3 to 6 focus groups (Krueger, 1994; Morgan, 1997; Onwuegbuzie, Dickinson, Leech, & Zoran, 2007)

For correlational, causal-comparative, and experimental research designs, the recommended sample sizes represent those needed to detect a medium (using Cohen's [1988] criteria), one-tailed statistically significant relationship or difference with .80 power at the 5% level of significance.

5. To estimate a proportion in a population:

Sample size =[(z-score)² × p(1-p)] ÷ (margin of error)²

The margin of error is what you are prepared to accept (usually between 1% and 10%);

The z-score, also called the z value, is found from statistical tables, and depends on the confidence interval chosen (90%, 95% and 99% are commonly used, so choose which one you want);

p is your estimate of what the proportion is likely to be. You can often estimate p from previous research, but if you cannot do that then use 0.5.

6. To estimate a population mean:
    Margin of error = t × (s ÷ square root of the sample size).
    Margin of error is what you are prepared to accept (usually between 1% and 10%)

    If the sample size is larger than about 30, t is equivalent to the z score, and available from statistical tables as before;

    s is the standard deviation, which is usually guessed, based on previous experience or another research.

7. By using the Calmorin's formula, the problem is solved as follows.

$$S_s = \frac{NV+[Se^2(1-p)]}{NSe+[V^2 \, p \,(1-p)]}$$

Where S_s stand for sample size; N, the population; V standard value (2.58) of 1 percent level of probability with 0.99 reliability level; Se, sampling error (0.01); and p, the largest possible proportion (0.50).

Example: Getting from a parameter of 900.

Given: N = 900; V = 2.58; Se = 0.01; p = 0.50

$$S_s = \frac{NV+[Se^2(1-p)]}{NSe+[V^2 \, p \,(1-p)]}$$

$$= \frac{900(2.58)+[(0.01)^2(1-0.50)]}{900(0.01)+[(2.58)^2(0.50)(1-0.50)]}$$

$$= \frac{2322+(0.0001)(0.50)}{9+(6.6564)(0.50)(0.50)}$$

$$= \frac{2322+0.00005}{9+6.6564(0.25)}$$

$$= \frac{2322+0.00005}{9+1.6641} = \mathbf{218}$$

Steps in sample design

While developing a sampling design, the researcher must pay attention to the following points:

1. **Type of universe:** The first step in developing any sample design is to clearly define the set of objects, technically called the Universe, to be studied. The universe can be finite or infinite. In finite universe the number of items is certain, but in case of an infinite universe the number of items is infinite, i.e., we cannot have any idea about the total number of items. The population of a city, the number of workers in a factory and the like are examples of finite universes, whereas the number of stars in the sky, listeners of a specific radio programme, throwing of a dice etc. are examples of infinite universes.

2. **Sampling unit:** A decision has to be taken concerning a sampling unit before selecting sample. Sampling unit may be a geographical one such as state, district, village, etc., or a construction unit such as house, flat, etc., or it may be a social unit such as family, club, school, etc., or it may be an individual. The researcher will have to decide one or more of such units that he has to select for his study.

3. **Source list:** It is also known as 'sampling frame' from which sample is to be drawn. It contains the names of all items of a universe (in case of finite universe only). If source list is not available, researcher has to prepare it. Such a list should be comprehensive, correct, reliable and appropriate. It is extremely important for the source list to be as representative of the population as possible.

4. **Size of sample:** This refers to the number of items to be selected from the universe to constitute a sample. This major problem before a researcher. The size of sample should neither be excessively large, nor too small. It should be optimum. An optimum sample is one which fulfills the requirements of efficiency, representativeness, reliability, and flexibility. While deciding the size of sample, researcher must determine the desired precision as also an acceptable confidence level for the estimate. The size of population variance needs to be considered as in case of larger variance usually a bigger sample is needed. The size of population must be kept in view for this also limits the sample size. The parameters of interest in a research study must be kept in view, while deciding the size of the sample. Costs too dictate the size of sample that we can draw. As such, budgetary constraint must invariably be taken into consideration when we decide the sample size.

5. **Parameters of interest:** In determining the sample design, one must consider the question of the specific population parameters which are of interest. For instance, we may be interested in estimating the proportion of persons with some characteristic in the population, or we may be interested in knowing some average or the other measure concerning the population. There

may also be important sub-groups in the population about whom we would like to make estimates. All this has a strong impact upon the sample design we would accept.

6. **Budgetary constraint:** Cost considerations, from practical point of view, have a major impact upon decisions relating to not only the size of the sample but also to the type of sample. This fact can even lead to the use of a non-probability sample.

7. **Sampling procedure:** Finally, the researcher must decide the type of sample he will use i.e., he must decide about the technique to be used in selecting the items for the sample. In fact, this technique or procedure stands for the sample design itself. There are several sample designs (explained in the pages that follow) out of which the researcher must choose one for his study. Obviously, he must select that design which, for a given sample size and for a given cost, has a smaller sampling error.

Criteria of Selecting a Sampling Procedure

In this context one must remember that two costs are involved in a sampling analysis viz., the cost of collecting the data and the cost of an incorrect inference resulting from the data. Researcher must keep in view the two causes of incorrect inferences viz., systematic bias and sampling error. Systematic bias results from errors in the sampling procedures, and it cannot be reduced or eliminated by increasing the sample size. At best the causes responsible for these errors can be detected and corrected. Usually, a systematic bias is the result of one or more of the following factors:

1. **Inappropriate sampling frame:** If the sampling frame is inappropriate i.e., a biased representation of the universe, it will result in a systematic bias.

2. **Defective measuring device:** If the measuring device is constantly in error, it will result in systematic bias. In survey work, systematic bias can result if the questionnaire or the interviewer is biased. Similarly, if the physical measuring device is defective there will be systematic bias in the data collected through such a measuring device.

3. **Non-respondents:** If we are unable to sample all the individuals initially included in the sample, there may arise a systematic bias. The reason is that in such a situation the likelihood of establishing contact or receiving a response from an individual is often correlated with the measure of what is to be estimated.

4. **Indeterminacy principle:** Sometimes we find that individuals act differently when kept under observation than what they do when kept in non-observed situations. For instance, if workers are aware that somebody is observing them in course of a work study based on which the average length of time to complete a task will be determined and accordingly the quota will be set for

piece work, they generally tend to work slowly in comparison to the speed with which they work if kept unobserved. Thus, the indeterminacy principle may also be a cause of a systematic bias.

5. **Natural bias in the reporting of data:** Natural bias of respondents in the reporting of data is often the cause of a systematic bias in many inquiries. There is usually a downward bias in the income data collected by government taxation department, whereas we find an upward bias in the income data collected by some social organization. People in general understate their incomes if asked about it for tax purposes, but they overstate the same if asked for social status or their affluence. Generally, in psychological surveys, people tend to give what they think is the 'correct' answer rather than revealing their true feelings.

Sampling errors are the random variations in the sample estimates around the true population parameters. Since they occur randomly and are equally likely to be in either direction, their nature happens to be of compensatory type and the expected value of such errors happens to be equal to zero. Sampling error decreases with the increase in the size of the sample, and it happens to be of a smaller magnitude in case of homogeneous population.

Sampling error can be measured for a given sample design and size. The measurement of sampling error is usually called the 'precision of the sampling plan'. If we increase the sample size, the precision can be improved. But increasing the size of the sample has its own limitations viz., a large sized sample increases the cost of collecting data and enhances the systematic bias. Thus, the effective way to increase precision is usually to select a better sampling design which has a smaller sampling error for a given sample size at a given cost. In practice, however, people prefer a less precise design because it is easier to adopt the same and also because of the fact that systematic bias can be controlled in a better way in such a design.

In brief, *while selecting a sampling procedure, researcher must ensure that the procedure causes a relatively small sampling error and helps to control the systematic bias in a better way.*

Characteristics of a good sample design

From what has been stated above, we can list down the characteristics of a good sample design as under:

a) Sample design must result in a truly representative sample.
b) Sample design must be such which results in a small sampling error.
c) Sample design must be viable in the context of funds available for the research study.
d) Sample design must be such so that systematic bias can be controlled in a better way.

e) Sample should be such that the results of the sample study can be applied, in general, for the universe with a reasonable level of confidence.

Sampling in Qualitative Research

Qualitative researchers typically make sampling choices that enable them to deepen understanding of whatever phenomenon it is that they are studying. Qualitative researchers typically employ when sampling as well as the various types of samples that qualitative researchers are most likely to use in their work.

Non-probability sampling represents a group of sampling techniques that help researchers to select units from a population that they are interested in studying. Collectively, these units form the sample that the researcher studies. A core characteristic of non-probability sampling techniques is that samples are selected based on the subjective judgement of the researcher, rather than random selection (i.e., probabilistic methods), which is the cornerstone of probability sampling techniques.

Nonprobability Sampling Design	Descriptions
1. **Purposive**	Researcher seeks out elements that meet specific criteria.
2. **Snowball**	Researcher relies on participant referrals to recruit new participants.
3. **Quota**	Researcher selects cases from within several different subgroups.
4. **Convenience**	Researcher gathers data from whatever cases happen to be convenient

Sampling in Quantitative Research

Quantitative researchers are often interested in being able to make generalizations about groups larger than their study samples. While there are certainly instances when quantitative researchers rely on nonprobability samples (e.g., when doing exploratory or evaluation research), quantitative researchers tend to rely on probability sampling techniques. The goals and techniques associated with probability samples differ from those of nonprobability samples.

Unlike nonprobability sampling, **probability sampling** refers to sampling techniques for which a person's (or event's) likelihood of being selected for membership in the sample is known. You might ask yourself why we should care about a study element's likelihood of being selected for membership in a researcher's sample. The reason is that, in most cases, researchers who use probability sampling techniques are aiming to identify a representative sample from which to collect data. A representative sample is one that resembles the population from which it was drawn in all the ways that are important for the research being conducted. If, for example, you wish to be able to say something about differences between men and women at the end of your study, you better make sure that your sample does not contain only women. That is a bit of an oversimplification, but the point with representativeness is that if your population varies in some way that is important to your study, your sample should contain the same sorts of variation.

Obtaining a representative sample is important in probability sampling because a key goal of studies that rely on probability samples is generalizability. In fact, generalizability is perhaps the key feature that distinguishes probability samples from nonprobability samples. **Generalizability** refers to the idea that a study's results will tell us something about a group larger than the sample from which the findings were generated. In order to achieve generalizability, a core principle of probability sampling is that all elements in the researcher's target population have an equal chance of being selected for inclusion in the study.

In research, this is the principle of **random selection**. Random selection is a mathematical process that we will not go into too much depth about here, but if you have taken or plan to take a statistics course, you will learn more about it there. The important thing to remember about random selection here is that, as previously noted, it is a core principal of probability sampling. If a researcher uses random selection techniques to draw a sample, he or she will be able to estimate how closely the sample represents the larger population from which it was drawn by estimating the sampling error. Sampling error is a statistical calculation of the difference between results from a sample and the actual parameters of a population.

Types of Probability Samples

There are a variety of probability samples that researchers may use. These include the following.

Probability Sampling Design	Descriptions
1. **Simple random**	Researcher randomly selects elements from sampling frame
2. **Systematic**	Researcher selects every kth element from sampling frame.
3. **Stratified**	Researcher creates subgroups then randomly selects elements from each subgroup.
4. **Cluster**	Researcher randomly selects clusters then randomly selects elements from selected clusters.

Sampling in Mixed Research

Mixed - Methods Sampling this is a sampling method that combines different types of sampling method into a single design. This is supported by the idea that the weakness of one method may be compensated by the strengths of the other method that is used. The use of mixed methods research design was spurred by application of two key concepts. "multi- method, multi - trait matrix and triangulation" which were introduced by Campbell & Fiske in 1959 (multi - method - multi- trait) and the four types of triangulation by Denzin (2009); "data triangulation, method logical triangulation, investigator triangulation, and theory triangulation" (in Daniel, 2012). Through the years, researchers have made adjustment in their sampling procedure as a response to change in technology, lifestyles, the legal environment, and nonresponse rates.

1. **Telephone - based sampling**. This is a sampling procedure that utilizes telephone numbers as sampling units. According to research, telephone surveys were the dominant survey methodology since the 1980s. There are two subtypes of telephone - based sampling, list - based sampling taken from telephone directories, list of employees, customers, etc. and random digit dialing (RDD). The random sampling procedure previously discussed can also be applied in the telephone - based sampling procedure.

2. **Web - based sampling.** In this sampling procedure, email addresses, website visits, and recruited users of the internet are utilized as sampling units. There are three categories of web - based sampling, namely list - based sampling, sampling of website visits, and sampling from recruited panels of potential participants in research projects.

3. **Address - based sampling (ABS)**. In this kind of sampling procedure, postal addresses are utilized as sampling units. The ABS sampling is used mostly in national surveys.

4. **Time - based sampling**. Units of time are used as sampling units in this type of sampling. This is used in studying repeated outcomes that vary a great deal over time. The units of time may be time of the day, days of the week, months of the year, or some other unit. The time intervals may be sampling units. The length of the interval would depend in part on the rate of occurrence of what is to be observed. Preparation for this type of sampling typically involves visits to the locations was the data will be collected, observing the density of the target population over time, and gathering information from informants. Using the information obtained, a sampling frame of time units is developed. Data might be collected several times per day at time periods selected using simple random sampling or systematic sampling, upon the occurrence of a specific event, or at specially scheduled time intervals. Subtypes of time- based sampling according to Daniel (2012) are experience sampling method, events sampling methodology; and the use of the time by employees' equipment, and facilities, known as work sampling. The variables that may be studied are social interaction, mood swings, levels of stress, or factors that have impact on work experiences and productivity.

5. **Space - based sampling**. This refers to a set of sampling procedures that utilize space as a sampling unit. This type of sampling is also referred to as area sampling, spatial sampling, location- based sampling, venue - based sampling and

facility - based sampling. The space may be geographical units or various locations or venues. It is the principal mode of sampling utilized in nationwide personal interview surveys, environmental sampling, and ecological sampling (Daniel, 2012).

Illustrative Example 1 of Sampling Design, Procedure and Technique.

> **Effectiveness of Claim, Evidence, and Reasoning as an Innovation to Develop Students' Scientific Argumentative Writing Skills (Samosa, 2020b)**
>
> **Sampling Technique**
>
> The researcher used purposive sampling. Under this method of drawing the sample, researcher selects the sampling units that meet the purpose or objective of the study. The subjects of the experiment are 20 Grade 11 Accountancy, Business and Management (ABM) Students from Graceville National High School in School Division of San Jose del Monte City, Bulacan. More so, the ratio of males to females among the participants depends on the number of enrollees this A.Y. 2019-2020.

Illustrative Example 2 of Sampling Design, Procedure and Technique.

> **Cultivating Research Culture: Capacity Building Program Toward Initiatives to Improve Teachers Self-Efficacy , Research Anxiety and Research Attitude (Samosa, 2021d)**
>
> **Sampling Technique**
>
> The researcher utilized the *Purposive sampling technique* and according to Samosa, et al, (2021), it is a form of non-probability sampling in which decisions concerning the individuals to be included in the sample are taken by the researcher, based upon a variety of criteria which may include specialist knowledge of the research issue, or capacity and willingness to participate in the research. The study involved the fifty (50) public secondary teachers composed of nine (9) Senior High School Teachers and forty - one (41) Junior High School Teachers in Graceville National High School who have not experienced in conducting action research.

Data Collection Methods

Data collection is a process of collecting information from all the relevant sources to find answers to the research problem, test the hypothesis and evaluate the outcomes. Data collection methods can be divided into two categories: secondary methods of data collection and primary methods of data collection.

1. **Secondary Data Collection Methods.** It is a type of data that has already been published in books, newspapers, magazines, journals, online portals etc. There is an abundance of data available in these sources about your research area in business studies, almost regardless of the nature of the research area. Therefore, application of appropriate set of criteria to select secondary data to be used in the study plays an important role in terms of increasing the levels of research validity and reliability. These criteria include, but not limited to date of publication, credential of the author, reliability of the source, quality of discussions, depth of analyses, the extent of contribution of the text to the development of the research area etc.

2. **Primary Data Collection Methods.**

   Primary data collection methods can be divided into two groups: quantitative and qualitative.

   a) **Quantitative data collection methods** are based in mathematical calculations in various formats. Methods of quantitative data collection and analysis include questionnaires with closed-ended questions, methods of correlation and regression, mean, mode and median and others. Quantitative methods are cheaper to apply, and they can be applied within shorter duration of time compared to qualitative methods. Moreover, due to a high level of standardization of quantitative methods, it is easy to make comparisons of findings.

   b) **Qualitative research methods**, on the contrary, do not involve numbers or mathematical calculations. Qualitative research is closely associated with words, sounds, feeling, emotions, colors and other elements that are non-quantifiable. Qualitative studies aim to ensure greater level of depth of understanding and qualitative data collection methods include interviews, questionnaires with open-ended questions, focus groups, observation, game or role-playing, case studies etc.

Research Instrumentation

Alongside with choosing the method of data collection is choosing the research instrument. Dagdag et. al (2006) defined research instruments as devices or tools which the research uses to gather answers to his research questions.

Researchers can choose the type of instruments to use based on their research question or objectives. There are two broad categories of instruments namely; *researchers - completed instruments* and *subject - completed instrument*. Examples are shown on the following table.

Researcher - completed Instruments	Subject - completed Instruments
Rating scales	Questionnaires
Interview schedules or guides	Self - checklists
Tally sheets	Attitude scales
Flowcharts	Personality inventories
Performance checklists	Achievement and Aptitude tests
Time - and - motion logs	Projective devices
Observation forms	Sociometric devices

Treece and Treece (1977), divided the research instrument or tools for gathering data in research are of two categories or kind.

Mechanical devices include almost all tools (such as microscope, telescopes, thermometers, rulers, and monitors) used in the physical sciences. In the social sciences and nursing, mechanical devices include such equipment as tape recorders, cameras, films, and video tapes. In addition, also included the laboratory tools and equipment used in experimental research in the chemical and biological sciences as in industry and agriculture.

Clerical tools are used when the researcher studies people and gathers data on the feelings, emotions, attitudes, and judgments of the subjects. Some of clerical tools are filled record, histories, case studies, questionnaires, and interviews schedules.

A critical potion of the research study is the instrument used to gather data. The validity of the findings and conclusion resulting from the statistical instruments will depend greatly on the characteristics of your instruments.

There are different ways of choosing for research instruments (Nalzaro, 2012):

1. Read professional journals to learn what kind of instruments are being used for similar studies, their format, style, and how they are used by the writers.
2. Read books that provide a description or an actual copy of various instruments for the reader.
3. Talk with other researchers who may know of certain tools they have developed for themselves or may have used tools developed by others.
4. Combine or adapt one or more tools used by other researchers.
5. Develop one's own instrument to fulfill a specific need.

According to Calderon (1993), the following are characteristics of a good research instruments:

1. The instrument must be valid and reliable.

2. It must be based upon the conceptual framework or what the researcher wants to find out.
3. It must gather data suitable for and relevant to the research topic.
4. It must gather data that would test the hypotheses or answer the questions under investigation.
5. It should be free from all kinds of bias.
6. It must contain only question or items that are unequivocal.
7. It must contain clear and definite directions to accomplish it.
8. If the instrument is a mechanical device, it must be of the best or latest model.
9. It must be accompanied by a good cover letter.
10. It must be accompanied, if possible, by letter of recommendation from a sponsor.

Data collection Instruments

Data collection is an important step in the research process. The instrument you choose to collect the data will depend on the type of data you plan on collecting (qualitative or quantitative) and how you plan to collect it.

Qualitative Data Collection

Qualitative research is a type of study carried out with a qualitative approach to understand the exploratory reasons and to assay how and why a specific program or phenomenon operates in the way it is working. A researcher can access numerous qualitative data collection methods that he/she feels are relevant. Qualitative data collection methods serve the primary purpose of collecting textual data for research and analysis. The collected research data is used to examine.

1. knowledge around a specific issue or a program, experience of people,
2. meaning and relationships, and
3. social norms and contextual or cultural practices demeaning people or impacting a cause.

The qualitative data is textual or non-numerical. It covers mostly the images, videos, texts, and written or spoken words by the people. researcher can opt for any digital data collection methods, like structured or semi-structured surveys, or settle for the traditional approach comprising individual interviews, group discussions, etc.

1. **Individual interview.** It is one of the most trusted, widely used, and most familiar qualitative data collection methods primarily because of its approach. An individual or a face-to-face interview is a direct conversation between two people with a specific structure and purpose. The interview questionnaire is designed in the manner to elicit the interviewee's knowledge or perspective related to a topic, program, or issue. At times, depending on the interviewer's

approach, the conversation can be unstructured or informal but focused on understanding the individual's beliefs, values, understandings, feelings, experiences, and perspectives of an issue. More often, the interviewer chooses to ask open-ended questions in individual interviews. If the interviewee selects answers from a set of given options, it becomes a structured, fixed response, or a biased discussion. The individual interview is an ideal qualitative data collection method, particularly when the researchers want highly personalized information from the participants. The individual interview is a notable method if the interviewer decides to probe further and ask follow-up questions to gain more insights.

2. **Qualitative surveys.** To develop an informed hypothesis, many researchers use qualitative surveys for data collection or to collect a piece of detailed information about a product or an issue. If you want to create questionnaires for collecting textual or qualitative data, then ask more open-ended questions. To answer such questions, the respondent has to write his/her opinion or perspective concerning a specific topic or issue. Unlike other qualitative data collection methods, online surveys have a wider reach wherein many people can provide you quality data that is highly credible and valuable.

   a) **Paper surveys**. The paper questionnaires are frequently used for qualitative data collection from the participants. The survey consists of short text questions, which are often open-ended. These questions' motive is to collect as much detailed information as possible in the respondents' own words. More often, the survey questionnaires are designed to collect standardized data hence used to collect responses from a larger population or large sample size.

   b) **Online surveys**. An online survey or a web survey is prepared using a prominent online survey software and either uploaded in a website or emailed to the selected sample size with a motive to collect reliable online data. Instead of writing down responses, the respondents use computers and keyboards to type their answers. With an online survey questionnaire, it becomes easier and smoother to collect qualitative data. In addition to that, online surveys have a wider reach, and the respondent is not pressurized to answer each question under the interviewer's supervision. One of the significant benefits that online surveys offer is that they allow the respondents to take the survey on any device, be it a desktop, tablet, or mobile.

3. **Focus group discussions.** Focus group discussions can also be considered a type of interview, but it is conducted in a group discussion setting. Usually, the focus group consists of 8 – 10 people (the size may vary depending on the researcher's requirement). The researchers ensure appropriate space is given to the participants to discuss a topic or issue in a context. The participants are allowed to either agree or disagree with each other's comments. With a

focused group discussion, researchers know how a particular group of participants perceives the topic. Researchers analyze what participants think of an issue, the range of opinions expressed, and the ideas discussed. The data is collected by noting down the variations or inconsistencies (if any exists) in the participants, especially in terms of belief, experiences, and practice. The participants of focused group discussions are selected based on the topic or issues for which the researcher wants actionable insights. Frequently, the qualitative data collected through focused group discussion is more descriptive and highly detailed.

4. **Observations.** It is one of the traditional qualitative data collection methods used by researchers to gather descriptive text data by observing people and their behavior at events or in their natural settings. In this method, the researcher is completely immersed in watching or seeing people by taking a participatory stance to take down notes. Aside from taking notes, different techniques such as videos, photographs, audio recordings, tangible items like artifacts, and souvenirs are also be used.

There are two main types of observation,

   a) **Covert:** In this method, the observer is concealed without letting anyone know that they are being observed. For example, a researcher studying the rituals of a wedding in nomadic tribes must join them as a guest and quietly see everything that goes around him.

   b) **Overt:** In this method, everyone is aware that they are being watched. For example, A researcher or an observer wants to study the wedding rituals of a nomadic tribe. To proceed with the research, the observer or researcher can reveal why he is attending the marriage and even use a video camera to shoot everything around him.

Observation is a useful qualitative data collection method, especially when research want to study the ongoing process, situation, or reactions on a specific issue related to the people being observed. Even when research want to understand people's behavior or their way of interaction in a particular community or demographic, researcher can rely on the observation data. Remember, if the researcher fails to get quality data through surveys, interviews, or group discussions, rely on observation. It is the best and trusted qualitative data collection method to generate qualitative data as it requires equal to no efforts from the participants.

Quantitative Data Collection

In contrast to qualitative data, quantitative data is everything about figures and numbers. Researchers often rely on quantitative data when they intend to quantify attributes, attitudes, behaviors, and other defined variables with a motive to either back or oppose the hypothesis of a specific phenomenon by contextualizing the data obtained via surveying or interviewing the study sample. As a researcher, you do have the option to opt either for data collection online or use traditional data collection methods via appropriate research. However, researcher need computational, statistical, and mathematical tools to derive results from the collected quantitative data.

A data that can be counted or expressed in numerical constitute the quantitative data. It is commonly used to study the events or levels of concurrence. And is collected through a structured questionnaire asking questions starting with "how much" or "how many." As the quantitative data is numerical, it represents both definitive and objective data. Furthermore, quantitative information is much sorted for statistical and mathematical analysis, making it possible to illustrate it in the form of charts and graphs.

Discrete and continuous are the two major categories of quantitative data where discreet data have finite numbers and the constant data values falling on a continuum possessing the possibility to have fractions or decimals. If research is conducted to find out the number of vehicles owned by the American household, then we get a whole number, which is an excellent example of discrete data. When research is limited to the study of physical measurements of the population like height, weight, age, or distance, then the result is an excellent example of continuous data.

Any traditional or online data collection method that helps in gathering numerical data is a proven method of collecting quantitative data.

1. **Experiment**. An experiment is a controlled study in which the researcher attempts to understand cause-and-effect relationships. The study is "controlled" in the sense that the researcher controls (1) how subjects are assigned to groups and (2) which treatments each group receives. In the analysis phase, the researcher compares group scores on some dependent variable. Based on the analysis, the researcher draws a conclusion about whether the treatment (independent variable) had a causal effect on the dependent variable.

2. **Census**. A census is a study that obtains data from every member of a population. In most studies, a census is not practical, because of the cost and/or time required.

3. **Rating scale** is defined as a closed-ended survey question used to represent respondent feedback in a comparative form for specific particular features/products/services. It is one of the most established question types for online and offline surveys where survey respondents are expected to rate an attribute or feature. Rating scale is a variant of the popular multiple-choice question which is widely used to gather information that provides relative information about a specific topic.

Validity and Reliability of Questionnaires: How to Check

For a questionnaire to be regarded as acceptable, it must possess two very important qualities which are reliability and validity. The former measures the consistency of the questionnaire while the latter measures the degree to which the results from the questionnaire agrees with the real world.

Reliability and validity are two very important qualities of a questionnaire. There are different statistical ways to measure the reliability and validity of your questionnaire. The statistical choice often depends on the design and purpose of the questionnaire.

Questionnaire Reliability. This also describes consistency. It is the extent to which that same questionnaire would produce the same results if the study were to be conducted again under the same conditions. Reliability is assessed by;

1. **Test-retest reliability.** This involves giving the questionnaire to the same group of respondents at a later point in time and repeating the research. Then, comparing the responses at the two time points. This type of reliability test has a disadvantage caused by memory effects. If the respondents respond to the questions in the way they remembered answering it the first time, it may provide the researcher with an artificial reliability. Thus, to reduce memory effects, the time between the first test and the retest should be increased.

2. **Inter-rater reliability.** Like the test-retest reliability, it is conducted under different conditions; the raters are different with one been systematically "harsher" than the other.

3. **Parallel form reliability**. Here, parallel equivalent forms of the questionnaire are developed (A and B). Both forms would be used to get the same information, but the questions would be constructed differently. Respondents are to fill both forms of questionnaires. Based on the assumption that both forms are interchangeable, the correlation of the 2 forms estimates the reliability of the questionnaire. A disadvantage of this checker is that it is expensive.

4. **Split-half reliability.** Split-half reliability measures the extent to which the questions all measure the same underlying construct. Here, the questions are split in two halves and then, the correlation of the scores on the scales from the two halves is calculated. Afterwards, the calculated correlation is run through the Spearman Brown formula.

Questionnaire Validity. This measures the degree of agreement of the results or conclusions gotten from the research questionnaire with the real world. Steps in validating a questionnaire include;

1. **Establish face validity.** First, have people who understand your topic go through your questionnaire. They should check if your questionnaire has captured the topic under investigation effectively. Secondly, get an

expert on questionnaire construction to check your questionnaire for double, confusing, and leading questions.

2. **Conduct a pilot test.** Sample size for pilot test varies. Researcher can decide to use a small sample size or a large one. For example, the researcher is going for 20 participants per question, if the researcher has questionnaire comprises 30 questions that means researcher would need a total of 600 respondents. After the respondents have filled out the form, researcher can then determine what questions are irrelevant and those that are not. Drop the irrelevant questions.

3. **Enter the pilot test in a spreadsheet.** Enter the data into a spreadsheet and clean the data. Have one person read the values while the other enters them. This would reduce mistakes that may happen if one person reads and enters the data. Using reversed code, negatively paraphrase questions to determine if the respondents answered recklessly. If the questions were answered correctly, their responses to the negative paraphrased questions will match similar positively phrased questions. If any inconsistency is found, the person's questionnaire should be tossed out. Check for minimum and maximum value for the entire data sets. If you are getting a response of 6 from a 5-point Likert style scale you have identified an error.

4. **Use principal component analysis (PCA).** This is used to identify underlying components. These components or factor loadings tell you what factors your questions measure. Factor loadings have values ranging from -1.0 to 1.0. When grouping factor loadings, researcher are advised to look for values that are ±0.60 or higher. researchers are advised not to attempt conducting principal component analysis if you are inexperienced.

5. **Check the internal consistency of questions loading onto the same factors.** This step is used to determine the correlation between questions loading onto the same factor and checks if the responses are consistent. A standard test is Cronbach's Alpha. Cronbach's Alpha. values range from 0-1.0. A value from 0.60-0.70 is also accepted. If you have a low value, you should consider removing a question; Cronbach's Alpha value may dramatically increase when you do so.

6. **Revise the questionnaire based on information from principal component analysis (PCA) and Cronbach's Alpha (CA).** Researcher can decide to analyze a particular question that does not adequately load onto a factor separately, especially because the researcher think the question is important. If the question that does not load onto a factor is unimportant, researcher can remove it from the questionnaire. Also, if removing a question increases the Cronbach's Alpha of a group question then, researcher can also remove

it from the factor loading group. If questionnaire undergoes major changes then researcher would have to conduct the pilot test again. A good questionnaire should be able to establish qualities of reliabilit and validity for it to be able to produce correct information concerning a particular topic. If a questionnaire used to conduct a study lacks these two very important characteristics, then the conclusion drawn from that particular study can be referred to as invalid. This often means, the study needs to be conducted again.

Illustrative Example of Instruments and Data Collection Procedure

Cultivating Research Culture: Capacity Building Program Toward Initiatives to Improve Teachers Self-Efficacy , Research Anxiety and Research Attitude (Samosa, 2021d)

Instruments

To determine the effectiveness of capacity building program towards research initiatives to improve the teachers' level of research self-efficacy, research anxiety and research attitude among the Faculty members of Graceville National High School, the researcher adapted the standardized survey questionnaires from the study of Rezai and Zamani-Miandashti (2015) and the research culture index assessment tools of Carina Joane V. Barroso and Marites M. Egar (2015).

The adapted standardized survey questionnaires consist of three parts. The first part is the research self-efficacy and it consist of fifteen item questionnaires that can be answered through four-point Likert scale, 1 – very low, 2 – Low, 3 – High and 4 – Very High.

Second part of the standardized survey questionnaires is the research anxiety which consist of fifteen item questionnaire that can be answered through four-point likert scale, 1 – Not agree, 2 – Slightly Agree, 3 – Agree and 4– Strongly agree.

The third of the survey questionnaire is the research attitude which consist of fifteen item questionnaires that can be answered through five-point likert scale, 1 - *Very Low Positive*, 2 – *Low Positive*, 3 - *High Positive*, 4 - *Very High Positive*. For the, the Research Culture Index is an assessment tool that determines the interaction of different elements that can affect the research culture of every organization. The tool is a result of the synergistic interactions among three dimensions namely, research competency, research process and research productivity.

Data Collection Procedure.

The researcher sought permission from the Schools Division Superintendent to conduct the study. Then, the researcher also secured permission from the school principal to administer the electronic survey questionnaire using google form. After which, the researcher orients the teacher's participants regarding the nature and purpose of the study. The researcher gave emphasis that confidentiality of information will be maintained all throughout the research process.

> The procedure of the study involved three phases: pre-assessment phase, the experiment phase, and the post-assessment phase. The Pre-Assessment Phase consists of a given training needs assessment for action research. The Implementation Phase is characterized by the researcher utilization of capacity building program towards research initiatives to improve the teachers' level of research self-efficacy, research anxiety and research attitude among the faculty members of Graceville National High School. The Post – Assessment Phase consists of a given post -assessment Likert scale questionnaire in order to assess the level of research self-efficacy, research anxiety and research attitude after the conduct of the study.
>
> After the implementation of Post – Assessment Phase, the researchers utilized the respondent's interviews to identify the perceived acceptability of using capacity building program towards research initiatives to improve the teachers' level of research self-efficacy, research anxiety and research attitude among the faculty members of Graceville National High School. Consequently, the researcher utilized the research culture index assessment tools to measure the level of the Research Culture in Graceville National High School.

Types of Data Analyzed in Research

Once the data collected, they must be analyzed before adequate interpretation can be made. Through analysis, a researcher can do four things:

1. Describe the data clearly,
2. Identify what is typical or atypical among data,
3. Bring to light differences, relationship, and other patters existent in the data; and
4. Answer research question or test hypotheses.

While data analysis aims at the same general goals, qualitative and quantitative are analyze differently.

Qualitative data are analyzed inductively, a thought process that utilizes logic to make sense of observation in which.

1. Observations are made of behavior, situations, interaction, objects, and environments.
2. Topics are identified from the observation and are
3. Scrutinized to discover patterns and categories, then
4. Conclusions are deduced from what is observed and are stated verbally and finally.
5. Those conclusions are used to answer research questions.

Quantitative data, on the hand are analyzed mathematically and the results are expressed in statistical analysis is used to –

1. Depict what is typical among the data.
2. Show degrees of difference or relationship between two or more variables; and

3. Determine the likelihood that the findings are real for the population as opposed to having occurred only by chance in the sample.

Methods of Analyzing Qualitative Data

Rebullida, et al. (1993), pointed out the there are different ways of analyzing qualitative data. Some of these methods are as follows: comparative, institutional, descriptive, historical, inductive, deductive, content analysis and theory -based analysis.

1. **Comparative methods of analysis.** This method relies on comparison and contrast in the analysis of a phenomenon, object, or situation. In using this method, the researcher has to remember that the things to compared or contrasted have to belong to same category or class. Moreover, there has to be a basis for comparison and contrast.

2. **Institutional method of analysis.** This method examines the characteristics, behavior patterns, roles, structure, functions, and even development of established or observed institutions. Institutional method of analysis can be done using history, description, comparison, and contrast.

3. **Descriptive Methods of Analysis.** In this method of analysis, the researcher has to present in greater details the nature or characteristics of the phenomena or situation being described. Data analysis in this approach may take any of the following forms: establishing categories or typologies; and determining sequence of events or patterns of behavior.

4. **Historical Analysis.** This can be utilized when the researcher is after explaining events or phenomena in the past so as to understand the present. In this method of analysis, the researcher needs to trace the events which had taken place and, at the same time, come up with a meaningful way of comprehending and interpreting these events. Generalizations in historical analysis are arrived at, based on the patterns of events that the researcher is able to discover.

5. **Inductive Analysis.** This method of analyzing qualitative data allows the pattern of thinking and reasoning that starts from specific to universal. The process starts from particular observation and ends up with generalization based on these specific observations.

6. **Deductive analysis.** This is the exact opposite of the inductive method of analysis. Here, the researcher has to begin with a general statement about a phenomenon, situation, or object. He ends up by providing details, particular or specific facts to support the said general statement.

7. **Content analysis.** This method is appropriate to use when the researcher is concerned about explaining the status of some phenomenon at a particular time or its development over a period of time using available documents.

Content analysis is also called documentary analysis. Sources of data for this method of analysis are as follows: records, reports, printed forms, letters, autobiographies, diaries, compositions, themes or other academic works, books, periodicals, bulletins or catalogues, syllabi, court decisions, pictures, films, and cartoons.

Methods of Analyzing Quantitative Data

Quantitative analysis is employed when the data to be analyzed are numerical or information which was assigned numerical values to facilitate counting, summarization, comparison, and generalization (Ardales, 1992). This type of analysis relies heavily on statistical techniques. Through statistics, the researcher can -

- Summarize data and reveal what is typical and atypical within a group.
- Show relative standing of individual in a group using percentile rankings, grade equivalents, age equivalents, and stanines;
- Show relationship among variables by means of statistical correlations;
- Show similarities and differences among groups with the use of the tests of differences;
- Identify error that is inherent in the selection of samples;
- Test for significance of findings; and
- Make other inferences about the population.

Analytic Procedures for Quantitative Data. There are five types of analytic procedure that a researcher can choose from, to answer the problems posed in his study namely: descriptive analysis, univariate analysis, bivariate analysis, multivariate analysis, and comparative analysis. Let us describe how each of these analytic procedures is done.

1. **Descriptive Analysis**. In this type of analysis, the researcher is only after describing the characteristics of the subjects under study. Data are usually analyzed to -
   - Identify the general characteristics of a group, with the use of descriptive statistics such as percentage, mean, median, and mode.
   - Determine differences in the group or how members of a group vary with reference to a given variable or factor being studied with the use of the standard deviation and coefficient of variation.

2. **Univariate analysis**. This type of analysis is employed when the researcher wants to analyze one variable or factor at a time. Univariate analysis relies heavily on the use of summary statistics, namely: measure of central tendency and measures if variability.
   - **Mean** is the most common average used to indicate the most typical response. It is computed by dividing the sum of the values by the

number of values or cases. It can only be subjected to arithmetical operations.

- **Median** is the middlemost value in an array, such that 50% are below it and 50% are above it. This is the appropriate average to use when the data are ordinal.
- **Mode** is the category or value with the greatest frequency of cases. It is the only acceptable indicator of the most typical case for data which are nominal or categorical.

Measures of variability are measures that reflect the amount of variation in the scores of a distribution. The most used measures for Univariate analysis are defined below.

- **Minimum and maximum values**. The minimum value indicates how far the spread toward the lower direction and the maximum value shows the extent of spread towards the upper direction from the average. These values describe the respondents or cases that represent the least and the most in whatever dimension is being measured.
- **Range**. It is simply the distance or difference between the maximum and minimum value, showing the total spread between extremes. It is the most unreliable measure of variability or dispersion as it is affected by extreme scores at either end of the distribution.
- **Standard deviation.** It is a measure of deviation or spread away from the mean. It is a single value that indicates the amount of dispersion in an array of scores.
- **Quartile deviation.** It is the appropriate measure of variability to employ when the median is the average used in describing a given distribution.

3. **Bivariate Analysis**. This type of analysis is used when the researcher is interested in probing into the relationship of two variables at a time. Bivariate analysis of relationship requires the use of Correlational statistics, such as Pearson's r, Spearman rho, Chi -square and other associational techniques.

4. **Multivariate Analysis**. This procedure for analyzing data is utilized when there is research question which cannot be responded using bivariate analysis. This analytic procedure permits the determination of the degree of relationship between one dependent variable and two or more independent variables simultaneously. The most used statistical tools for multivariate analysis are multiple regression analysis and multiple classification analysis.

5. **Comparative analysis.** When research participants must be compared based on certain variables being studied, comparative analysis is appropriate to use. This type of analysis requires the use of statistical tests of significant difference, like the t- test, critical ratio test and analysis of variance (ANOVA).

Effectiveness of Claim, Evidence, and Reasoning as an Innovation to Develop Students' Scientific Argumentative Writing Skills (Samosa, 2020b)

Data Analysis

The researcher utilized the weighted mean using a "five – point – scales or Likert Scale of Attitude Survey and the pre-post intervention survey and given weight as follows:

Rate	Verbal Interpretation		Interval Range
	Attitude Survey	**Pre-post intervention survey**	
5	Very Low Positive (VP)	Very comfortable (VC)	4.51– 5.00
4	Low positive (LP)	Comfortable (C)	3.51 – 4.50
3	Neutral (N)	Somewhat comfortable (SM)	2.51 – 3.50
2	Positive attitude (PA)	Not very comfortable (NVC)	1.51 – 2.50
1	High positive attitude (HPA)	Not comfortable (NC)	1.00 – 1.50

These were used to determine the student confidence and attitudes toward writing in science and learning in science, and the nature of science using CER Innovation.

To identify the level of the scientific argumentative writing skills of the students, the researcher will utilize the weighted mean using a four– point – rating scale rubric adapted from McNeill and Krajcik (2008) and given weight as follows:

Rate	Interval Range	Level
4	3.50 – 4.00	Excelling (E)
3	2.50 – 3.49	Proficient (P)
2	1.50 – 2. 49	Developing (D)
1	1.00 – 1.49	Not demonstrating (NT)

To determine whether there are significant differences in the pre-test and post-test scores, the t test for mean difference were utilized.

The participants' interviews was transcribed, coded, and analyzed to identify the perspectives/ themes and their categorization. Furthermore, the qualitative data, thematic analysis will be used following the 6 phases which was proposed by Clarke and Brawn (2006) as cited by Prieto et. al (2017). These six phases are as follows:
1. Familiarizing oneself with the data gathered;
2. Generating initial codes that involve the production of initial codes from the data;
3. Searching for themes which re-focuses on the analyses at the broader level of themes and collating all the relevant coded extracts within the identified themes;
4. Reviewing themes which involve two levels of reviewing themes;
5. Defining and naming the themes and involves the themes to be presented for analysis; and
6. Producing the report which involves the final analysis and writes up of the report.

Cooperative Learning Approach as Innovation to Improve Students' Academic Achievement and Attitude in Teaching Biology (Samosa, 2021e)

Statistical Treatment

A. Pre experimental data
The following statistical tool were used to determine the entry level of student and to determine they were comparable in terms of achievement in biology, and in their attitudes towards learning in Biology.

1. Mean. This was used to determine the average performance of each group in the achievement test and attitude test.
2. t – test for independent means. To determine whether there are significant differences in the achievement the t test for independent was utilized.
3. F – Test. This is used to compare the pre – post experiment attitude of the groups and to determine if there was no significant difference exists between the two groups.

B. Post Experimental data
4. t – Test for dependent means. This statistical measure is used to determine the significant gains made between the pretest and post test score of two groups. The test, likewise, used the 0.05 level of significance.
5. t – Test for independent means. This is used to determine whether the two groups posted significant difference in their achievement in terms of their achievement scores after the experiment.

Illustrative Example 3 of Data Analysis

CoSIM (Comics cum SIM): An Innovative Material in Teaching Biology (Samosa, 2021f)

Data Analysis

In analyzing the data, descriptive and inferential statistics will be employed. mean used to determine the average performance of pre-posttest and attitude test. The t-test will be employed to determine if there is a significant difference between the pretest-posttest before and after the implementation of CoSIM (Comics cum SIM) as an innovative material in teaching photosynthesis. More so, pearson – product moment correlation coefficient will be used to indicate the significant relationship of the respondent's academic performance and the level of academic performance and the attitudes towards exposure to CoSIM.

Assessment Tasks

I. **Direction:** Identify the sampling method in the given situation.

1. Rainier wants to survey principals and supervisor in country X. all in all, there are 12,000 principals and 24,000 supervisors in the country. Rainier decided to select 350 from total target population as participants in his study.
2. Darwin is conducting research on why students frequently play *Pokemon Go.* Darwin asked his classmate who frequently play game to bring with him five of his friends who also frequently *Pokemon Go.*
3. Paopao target population for her study are employees from the top 500 corporation in the Philippines. Because there are too many employees in these corporations, she decided to randomly select ten corporations and use all of their employees as participants in her study.
4. Restoy wants to find out the emotional challenges experienced by teenage mothers. He interviewed teenagers who are single mothers, aged 13 to 19, and living with their parents.
5. Valerie wants to know how student – athletes cope with academic demands. She went to the school gymnasium where the athletes usually practice. She stood at the entrance of gymnasium and started interviewing the student -athletes as they entered.
6. Timothy wants to know if the new curriculum has an effect on the academic performance of science students. He took the list of all students in his school and selected every 8th in the class list as participants.
7. Yang wants to study the online behavior of honor students in her school. There were 80 honors students in her school – tens from Grade 7; 15 from Grade 8; 20 from Grade 9; five from Grade 10; ten from Grade 11; 20 from Grade 12. Yang decided to get two participants from Grade 7, three from Grade 8; four from Grade 9; one from Grade 10; two from Grade 11, and four from Grade 12. Yang used her own judgement in selecting the participants.
8. Ella's study aims to determine the relationship between intelligence quotient and the language proficiency of students. These are 105,000 students in her target population. Of these, 15% have high proficiency, 65% have average proficiency, and 20% have low proficiency. She decided to utilize a sample size of 400 participants from the target population. This is proportional to the total number of members in each group of the population.
9. A researcher wishes to conduct a survey of research staff at the University of Kent, to investigate their views about proposed changes to the library opening times. She obtains a list of all of the university's

research staff, and selects 100 people from the list using a random number table.

10. In a survey of hospital out-patients' views about the quality of service they receive from a hospital, researchers wanted to canvas an equal amount of women and men. During one particular week 200 women and 200 men were asked to fill in a questionnaire.

II. **Direction:** Choose the letter of the correct answer.

1. Which of the following is not an aspect of a qualitative study design?
   a) The distinction between study design and data collection method is less defined.
   b) The design is based on deductive logic, flexible and emergent in nature.
   c) The design selects the participants through an open frame of enquiry.
   d) The design is specific, well-structured and sequential.

2. Some commonly used study designs in quantitative research are examined from three different perspectives, which one is not one of them?
   a) The reference period of the study.
   b) The resources the researcher has available.
   c) The number of contacts with the study population.
   d) The nature of the investigation

3. The study population is _________________.
   a) The way elements are selected for the sample.
   b) The number of elements from which information is obtained.
   c) Findings based on the information obtained.
   d) The group of interest for the study from which the sample is selected from.

4. Which of the following is not a non-random sampling method?
   a) Convenience sampling
   b) Purposive sampling
   c) Cluster sampling
   d) Quota sampling

5. Systematic sampling ________________.
   a) Needs a list of all elements in the study population.
   b) Uses the researcher's judgment as to the ability of the respondents to contribute to the research.
   c) Is based on convenience in accessing the sample population.
   d) Is none of the above.

6. Which of the following features are considered as critical in qualitative research?
   a) Collecting data with the help of standardized research tools.

b) Design sampling with probability sample techniques.
c) Collecting data with bottom-up empirical evidence.
d) Gathering data with top-down schematic evidence.

7. Research intends to explore the result of possible factors for the organization of effective mid-day meal interventions. Which research design will be most appropriate for this study?
   a) Descriptive survey design
   b) Historical design
   c) Ex-post facto design
   d) Experimental design

8. A researcher is interested in studying the prospects of a particular political party in an urban area. So, what tool should he prefer for the study?
   a) Rating Scale
   b) Interview
   c) Questionnaire
   d) Schedule

9. The conclusions/findings of which type of research cannot be generalized to other situations?
   a) Casual Comparative Research Design
   b) Narrative Research Design
   c) Descriptive Research Design
   d) Experimental Research Design

10. Action-research can be understood as ____________
    a) A longitudinal research
    b) An applied research
    c) A kind of research being carried out to solve a specific problem.
    d) All of the above

Performance Tasks.

Design and Make a Research Methodology

Direction: Focusing on the research problem that you developed in previous chapters, design or formulate a plan for research Methodology to answer your questions. Make sure to include a description of each of the components of the research methodology.

1. **Research Design**
   - Indicate the reason why you used qualitative, quantitative, or mixed research as your research methods.
   - Describe your chosen research design.
2. **Population and sample**
   - Describe the population in the study (including size, if it can be determined, and how it will be identified).
   - Identify whether sampling design for this population is single stage or multistage (called cluster sampling).
   - Identify how individual will be selected.
   - Describe in details the sampling procedure (the sample size and how the size was determined; the procedure for selecting the sample; the sampling frame, etc).
3. **Instrumentation/ Research Instrument (s).**
   - Identify the instrument to be used in the study, whether it is a self-designed, a modified instrument, or an intact instrument developed by someone else.
   - If you plan to use an existing instrument, describe the established validity and reliability and scales of the instruments, includes sample items to inform the readers of the actual items used.
   - Indicate the major contents sections in the instruments, such as the cover letter, items and closing instructions.
   - Discuss plans for pilot testing or field testing the instrument and provide a rationale for this procedure.
4. **Data Gathering Procedure.**
   - Indicate the reasons why a survey is the preferred type of data collection method for the study. (quantitative research. Specify the form of data collection (mailed to respondent in the sample, administered in a face -to -face interview, or gathered through telephone interviews). For a mailed survey, electronic survey , identify to be taken in administering and following up the survey to obtain a high response rate.
   - Identify the parameters for data collection (qualitative research)

a) The actors – who will be observed or interviewed and how will they be sampled.
b) The events – what the actors will be observed doing or interviewed about; and
c) The process – (the evolving nature of events undertaken by the actors within the setting.

- Provide a rationale for the data collection procedure (e.g., costs, availability/time, and convenience).
- Discuss actions to be taken to gain entry to the setting and to secure permission to study the informants or situation. Include a justification why the site of study has been chosen, a description of what will be accomplished during the research study, the impact of the research -related activities, and how the results will be reported? (qualitative research)
- Indicate potential or anticipated sensitive ethical difficulties or problems such as maintaining confidentially of data, preserving the anonymity of informants, and using research for intended purposes.

5. **Data Recording Procedure (Qualitative Research)**
   - Describe your plan for data recording. What is to be recorded? How will you have recorded it?

6. **Variables**
   - Indicates the rating scales to be used to measure the variables of the study.

7. **Data Analysis**
   - Indicates that information about the number of returns and nonreturns of the survey will be reported.
   - Discuss the methods by which response bias will be determined.
   - Report that a descriptive analysis of all independent and dependent variables in the study will be conducted. (quantitative research)
   - Describe the plan for making sense and interpreting data collected. Is there a coding procedure to be applied, and why?
   - If you are building your own scales in an instrument, discuss how survey items will be combined into scales on the independent and dependent dimensions. (quantitative research)
   - Identify the statistics to be used to compare groups or relate variables and answer the research questions or objectives of the study. (quantitative research).

Rubric for Writing the Research Methodology

Criteria	Excellent 15-20	Good 8-14	Poor 1-7
Research Design	Appropriate design chosen; good definition of the design; demonstrates familiarity with the defining features of the design	Appropriate design chosen; good definition of the design but lacks complete understanding of the key characteristics of the design chosen.	Inappropriate research design chosen; lacks a clear articulation of the rationale for selecting the design; inaccurate characterization of the design.
Sampling and Sampling Procedure	Elaborate description of the sample and sampling procedure	Lacks detailed description of the sample and sampling procedure.	Shows no familiarity with sampling and sampling procedure.
Variables	Clear operational definitions of variables, clear and sufficient indicators for the variables.	Clear operational definitions of variables but insufficient indicators used for the variables	Lacks clear operational definitions of variables, inaccurate indicators for variables.
Instruments	Elaborate description of instruments used.	Instruments for the study not sufficiently described and justified.	Poor description of instruments for the study.
Data collection Procedure	Four parameters for data collection are clearly described: clear description and justification for data collection procedures.	Four parameters for data collection are not sufficiently described and justified.	Four parameter for data collection, are missing: no clear indication of data collection procedures.
Data analysis procedures	Clear plan for analyzing and interpreting data.	Insufficiently clear articulation of data analysis and interpretation procedures.	No clear indication of data analysis procedures.

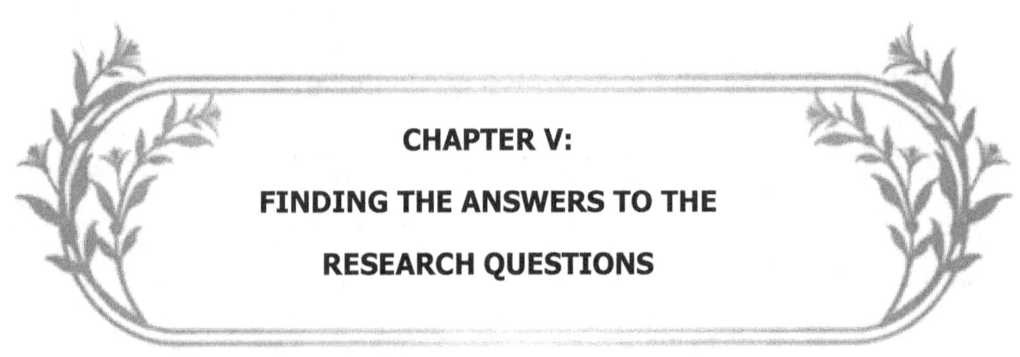

LEARNING OBJECTIVE
At the end of this chapter, students should be able to gathers and analyzes data with intellectual honesty using suitable techniques

Thematic Analysis for Qualitative Data

Thematic analysis is a flexible data analysis plan that qualitative researchers use to generate themes from interview data. According to Braun & Clarke (2006), It is best thought of as an umbrella term for a set of approaches for analyzing qualitative data that share a focus on identifying themes (patterns of meaning) in qualitative data.

There are six phases of Thematic Analysis.

1. **Familiarization with the data.** This phase involves reading and re-reading the data, to become immersed and intimately familiar with its content.
2. **Coding**. This phase involves generating succinct labels (codes) that identify important features of the data that might be relevant to answering the research question. It involves coding the entire dataset, and after that, collating all the codes and all relevant data extracts, together for later stages of analysis.
3. **Generating initial themes.** This phase involves examining the codes and collated data to identify significant broader patterns of meaning (potential themes). It then involves collating data relevant to each candidate theme, so that you can work with the data and review the viability of each candidate theme.
4. **Reviewing themes.** This phase involves checking the candidate themes against the dataset, to determine that they tell a convincing story of the data, and one that answers the research question. In this phase, themes are typically refined, which sometimes involves them being split, combined,

or discarded. In this approach, themes are defined as pattern of shared meaning underpinned by a central concept or idea.

5. **Defining and naming themes**. This phase involves developing a detailed analysis of each theme, working out the scope and focus of each theme, determining the 'story' of each. It also involves deciding on an informative name for each theme.

6. **Writing up.** This final phase involves weaving together the analytic narrative and data extracts and contextualizing the analysis in relation to existing literature.

There are different ways Thematic Analysis can be approached – within our reflexive approach all variations are possible:

1. An **inductive** way – coding and theme development are directed by the content of the data.

2. A **deductive** way – coding and theme development are directed by existing concepts or ideas.

3. A **semantic** way – coding and theme development reflect the explicit content of the data.

4. A **latent** way – coding and theme development report concepts and assumptions underpinning the data.

5. A **(critical) realist** or essentialist way – focuses on reporting an assumed reality evident in the data.

6. A **constructionist** way – focuses on looking at how a certain reality is created by the data.

More inductive, semantic and (critical) realist approaches tend to cluster together, ditto more deductive, latent and constructionist ones. In reality, the separation is not always that rigid. What is vitally important is that your analysis is theoretically coherent and consistent.

A 15-point checklist of criteria for good thematic analysis (Braun & Clarke, 2006):

Process	Criteria
Transcription	1. The data have been transcribed to an appropriate level of detail, and the transcripts have been checked against the tapes for 'accuracy'
Coding	2. Each data item has been given equal attention in the coding process.
	3. Themes have not been generated from a few vivid examples (an anecdotal approach), but instead the coding process has been thorough, inclusive, and comprehensive.
	4. All relevant extracts for all each theme have been collated.
	5. Themes have been checked against each other and back to the original data set
	6. Themes are internally coherent, consistent, and distinctive.
	7. Data have been analyzed / interpreted, made sense of / rather than just paraphrased or described.

Analysis	8. Analysis and data match each other / the extracts illustrate the analytic claims.
	9. Analysis tells a convincing and well-organized story about the data and topic.
	10. A good balance between analytic narrative and illustrative extracts is provided.
Overall	11. Enough time has been allocated to complete all phases of the analysis adequately, without rushing a phase or giving it a once-over-lightly
Written report	12. The assumptions about, and specific approach to, thematic analysis are clearly explicated.
	13. There is a good fit between what you claim you do, and what you show you have done / ie, described method and reported analysis are consistent.
	14. The language and concepts used in the report are consistent with the epistemological position of the analysis.
	15. The researcher is positioned as active in the research process; themes do not just 'emerge'.

Content Analysis for Qualitative Data.

Content analysis is a research tool used to determine the presence of certain words, themes, or concepts within some given qualitative data (i.e. text). Using content analysis, researchers can quantify and analyze the presence, meanings and relationships of such certain words, themes, or concepts. It is any technique for making inferences by systematically and objectively identifying special characteristics of messages.

Uses of Content Analysis

1. Identify the intentions, focus or communication trends of an individual, group or institution.
2. Describe attitudinal and behavioral responses to communications.
3. Determine psychological or emotional state of persons or groups.
4. Reveal international differences in communication content.
5. Reveal patterns in communication content.
6. Pre-test and improve an intervention or survey prior to launch.
7. Analyze focus group interviews and open-ended questions to complement quantitative data.

Types of Content Analysis

There are two general types of content analysis: conceptual analysis and relational analysis. Conceptual analysis determines the existence and frequency of concepts in a text. Relational analysis develops the conceptual analysis further by examining the relationships among concepts in a text. Each type of analysis may lead to different results, conclusions, interpretations and meanings.

Conceptual Analysis

Typically, people think of conceptual analysis when they think of content analysis. In conceptual analysis, a concept is chosen for examination and the analysis involves quantifying and counting its presence. The main goal is to examine the occurrence of selected terms in the data. Terms may be explicit or implicit. Explicit terms are easy to identify. Coding of implicit terms is more complicated: you need to decide the level of implication and base judgments on subjectivity (issue for reliability and validity). Therefore, coding of implicit terms involves using a dictionary or contextual translation rules or both.

To begin a conceptual content analysis, first identify the research question and choose a sample or samples for analysis. Next, the text must be coded into manageable content categories. This is basically a process of selective reduction. By reducing the text to categories, the researcher can focus on and code for specific words or patterns that inform the research question.

General steps for conducting a conceptual content analysis:

1. **Decide the level of analysis: word, word sense, phrase, sentence, themes**.
2. **Decide how many concepts to code for develop pre-defined or interactive set of categories or concepts**. Decide either: A. to allow flexibility to add categories through the coding process, or B. to stick with the pre-defined set of categories.
   - Option A allows for the introduction and analysis of new and important material that could have significant implications to one's research question.
   - Option B allows the researcher to stay focused and examine the data for specific concepts.
3. **Decide whether to code for existence or frequency of a concept. The decision changes the coding process**.
   - When coding for the existence of a concept, the researcher would count a concept only once if it appeared at least once in the data and no matter how many times it appeared.
   - When coding for the frequency of a concept, the researcher would count the number of times a concept appears in a text.

4. **Decide on how you will distinguish among concepts.**
   - Should text be coded exactly as they appear or coded as the same when they appear in different forms? For example, "dangerous" vs. "dangerousness". The point here is to create coding rules so that these word segments are transparently categorized in a logical fashion. The rules could make all of these word segments fall into the same category, or perhaps the rules can be formulated so that the researcher can distinguish these word segments into separate codes.
   - What level of implication is to be allowed? Words that imply the concept or words that explicitly state the concept? For example, "dangerous" vs. "the person is scary" vs. "that person could cause harm to me". These word segments may not merit separate categories, due the implicit meaning of "dangerous".
5. **Develop rules for coding your texts**. After decisions of steps 1-4 are complete, a researcher can begin developing rules for translation of text into codes. This will keep the coding process organized and consistent. The researcher can code for exactly what he/she wants to code. Validity of the coding process is ensured when the researcher is consistent and coherent in their codes, meaning that they follow their translation rules. In content analysis, obeying by the translation rules is equivalent to validity.
6. **Decide what to do with irrelevant information**. should this be ignored (e.g. common English words like "the" and "and"), or used to reexamine the coding scheme in the case that it would add to the outcome of coding?
7. **Code the text.** This can be done by hand or by using software. By using software, researchers can input categories and have coding done automatically, quickly and efficiently, by the software program. When coding is done by hand, a researcher can recognize error far more easily (e.g. typos, misspelling). If using computer coding, text could be cleaned of errors to include all available data. This decision of hand vs. computer coding is most relevant for implicit information where category preparation is essential for accurate coding.
8. **Analyze your results.** Draw conclusions and generalizations where possible. Determine what to do with irrelevant, unwanted or unused text: reexamine, ignore, or reassess the coding scheme. Interpret results carefully as conceptual content analysis can only quantify the information. Typically, general trends and patterns can be identified.

Relational Analysis

Relational analysis begins like conceptual analysis, where a concept is chosen for examination. However, the analysis involves exploring the relationships between concepts. Individual concepts are viewed as having no inherent meaning and rather the meaning is a product of the relationships among concepts.

To begin a relational content analysis, first identify a research question and choose a sample or samples for analysis. The research question must be focused so the concept types are not open to interpretation and can be summarized. Next, select text for analysis. Select text for analysis carefully by balancing having enough information for a thorough analysis so results are not limited with having information that is too extensive so that the coding process becomes too arduous and heavy to supply meaningful and worthwhile results.

There are three subcategories of relational analysis to choose from prior to going on to the general steps.

    a) **Affect extraction**. an emotional evaluation of concepts explicit in a text. A challenge to this method is that emotions can vary across time, populations, and space. However, it could be effective at capturing the emotional and psychological state of the speaker or writer of the text.

    b) **Proximity analysis**. an evaluation of the co-occurrence of explicit concepts in the text. Text is defined as a string of words called a "window" that is scanned for the co-occurrence of concepts. The result is the creation of a "concept matrix", or a group of interrelated co-occurring concepts that would suggest an overall meaning.

    c) **Cognitive mapping**. a visualization technique for either affect extraction or proximity analysis. Cognitive mapping attempts to create a model of the overall meaning of the text such as a graphic map that represents the relationships between concepts.

General steps for conducting a relational content analysis:

1. **Determine the type of analysis**. Once the sample has been selected, the researcher needs to determine what types of relationships to examine and the level of analysis: word, word sense, phrase, sentence, themes.
2. **Reduce the text to categories and code for words or patterns**. A researcher can code for existence of meanings or words.
3. **Explore the relationship between concepts**. once the words are coded, the text can be analyzed for the following:
   - Strength of relationship: degree to which two or more concepts are related.
   - Sign of relationship: are concepts positively or negatively related to each other?

- Direction of relationship: the types of relationship that categories exhibit. For example, "X implies Y" or "X occurs before Y" or "if X then Y" or if X is the primary motivator of Y.

4. **Code the relationships**. a difference between conceptual and relational analysis is that the statements or relationships between concepts are coded.
5. **Perform statistical analyses**. explore differences or look for relationships among the identified variables during coding.
6. **Map out representations**. such as decision mapping and mental models.

Choosing the Appropriate Statistical Test and Techniques for Analyzing Quantitative Data.

In statistics, for each of the specific situation, statistical methods are available for analysis and interpretation of the data. To select the appropriate statistical method, one need to know the assumption and conditions of the statistical methods, so that proper statistical method can be selected for data analysis. Two main statistical methods are used in data analysis: ***descriptive statistics***, which summarizes data using indexes such as mean and median and another is ***inferential statistics***, which draw conclusions from data using statistical tests such as student's t-test. **Selection of appropriate statistical method depends on the following three things**:

1. **Aim and objective of the study**. Selection of statistical test depends upon our aim and objective of the study. Suppose our objective is to find out the predictors of the outcome variable, then regression analysis is used while to compare the means between two independent samples, unpaired samples t-test is used.
2. **Type and distribution of the data used**. For the same objective, selection of the statistical test is varying as per data types. For the nominal, ordinal, discrete data, we use nonparametric methods while for continuous data, parametric methods as well as nonparametric methods are used. For example, in the regression analysis, when our outcome variable is categorical, logistic regression while for the continuous variable, linear regression model is used. The choice of the most appropriate representative measure for continuous variable is dependent on how the values are distributed. If continuous variable follows normal distribution, mean is the representative measure while for non-normal data, median is considered as the most appropriate representative measure of the data set. Similarly, in the categorical data, proportion (percentage) while for the ranking/ordinal data, mean ranks are our representative measure. In the inferential statistics, hypothesis is constructed using these measures and further in the hypothesis testing, these measures are used to compare between/among the groups to calculate significance level.

3. **Nature of the observations (paired/unpaired).** Another important point in selection of the statistical test is to assess whether data is paired (same subjects are measures at different time points or using different methods) or unpaired (each group have different subject). For example, to compare the means between two groups, when data is paired, paired samples t-test while for unpaired (independent) data, independent samples t-test is used.

Concept of Parametric and Nonparametric Methods

Inferential statistical methods fall into two possible categorizations: parametric and nonparametric. All type of statistical methods those are used to compare the means are called parametric while statistical methods used to compare other than means (ex-median/mean ranks/proportions) are called ***nonparametric methods***. ***Parametric tests*** rely on the assumption that the variable is continuous and follow approximate normally distributed. When data is continuous with non-normal distribution or any other types of data other than continuous variable, nonparametric methods are used. Fortunately, the most frequently used parametric methods have nonparametric counterparts. This can be useful when the assumptions of a parametric test are violated, and researcher can choose the nonparametric alternative as a backup analysis.

Parametric tests

1. **Mean** - The mean is more commonly called the average; however, this is incorrect if "mean" is taken in the specific sense of "arithmetic mean" as there are different types of averages: the mean, median, and mode.
2. **Standard Deviation** - The standard deviation measures the spread of the data about the mean value. It is useful in comparing sets of data, which may have the same mean but a different range.
3. **t test** - The t-test assesses whether the means of two groups are statistically different from each other. This analysis is appropriate whenever you want to compare the means of two group.
4. **Analysis of variance (ANOVA)** – This is used to test hypotheses about differences between two or more means as in the t-test, however when there are more than two means, analysis of variance can be used to test differences for significance without increasing the error rate (Type I).
5. **Pearson correlation** – This is a common measure of the correlation between two variables. A correlation of +1 means that there is a perfect

positive linear relationship between variables. A correlation of -1 means that there is a perfect negative linear relationship between variables.

6. **Regression (linear and non linear)** - A technique used for the modelling and analysis of numerical data. Regression can be used for prediction (including forecasting of time-series data), inference, hypothesis testing, and modelling of causal relationships.

Non-parametric tests

1. **Median** - The median is the middle of a distribution: half the scores are above the median and half are below the median. The median is less sensitive to extreme scores than the mean and this makes it a better measure than the mean for highly skewed distributions. The median income is usually more informative than the mean income for example.

2. **Interquartile range** - The interquartile range (IQR) is the distance between the 75th percentile and the 25th percentile. The IQR is essentially the range of the middle 50% of the data. Because it uses the middle 50%, the IQR is not affected by outliers or extreme values.

3. **Spearman correlation** - Spearman's Rank Correlation is a technique used to test the direction and strength of the relationship between two variables. In other words, it's a device to show whether any one set of numbers has an effect on another set of numbers.

4. **Chi - square test.** It is used as an inferential statistics for nominal or categorical data. This is the most versatile among the test of statistical significance, as can be both as a test of relationship or test of difference. When employed as a test of relationship, it is called a test of independence. When used as a test of difference, it is considered a test of homogeneity.

5. **Wilcoxon test -** The Wilcoxon test compares two paired groups of data. It calculates the differences between each set of pairs and analyses the list of differences.

6. **Mann-Whitney test** – it is a non-parametric test for assessing whether two samples of observations come from the same distribution, testing the null hypothesis that the probability of an observation from one population exceeds the probability of an observation in a second population.

7. **Kruskal-Wallis test -** A non-parametric method for testing equality of population medians among groups, using a one-way analysis of variance by ranks.

8. **Friedman test -** it is a nonparametric test that compares three or more paired groups.

Parametric and their Alternative Nonparametric Methods

Description	Parametric Methods	Nonparametric Methods
Descriptive statistics	Mean, Standard deviation	Median, Interquartile range
Sample with population (or hypothetical value)	One sample t-test ($n <30$) and One sample Z-test ($n \geq30$)	One sample Wilcoxon signed rank test
Two unpaired groups	Independent samples t-test (Unpaired samples t-test)	Mann Whitney U test/Wilcoxon rank sum test
Two paired groups	Paired samples t-test	Related samples Wilcoxon signed-rank test
Three or more unpaired groups	One-way ANOVA	Kruskal-Wallis H test
Degree of linear relationship	Pearson's correlation coefficient	Spearman rank correlation coefficient
Predict one outcome variable by at least one independent variable	Linear regression model	Nonlinear regression model/Log linear regression model on log normal data.

Statistical Methods to Compare the Proportions

The statistical methods used to compare the proportions are considered nonparametric methods and these methods have no alternative parametric methods.

Pearson Chi-square test and Fisher exact test is used to compare the proportions between two or more independent groups.

To test the change in proportions between two paired groups, **McNemar test** is used while **Cochran Q test** is used for the same objective among three or more paired groups.

Z test for proportions is used to compare the proportions between two groups for independent as well as dependent groups.

Statistical Methods to Compare the Proportions

Description	Statistical Methods	Data Type
Test the association between two categorical variables (Independent groups)	Pearson Chi-square test/Fisher exact test	Variable has ≥2 categories
Test the change in proportions between 2/3 groups (paired groups)	McNemar test/Cochrane Q test	Variable has 2 categories

Comparisons between proportions	Z test for proportions	Variable has 2 categories

Summarizes the four levels of measurement scales and the appropriate statistics for each level.

Scales of measurement	Relations being defined	Appropriate statistical test to be used	Examples of statistical that can be used.
Nominal	Equivalence	Nonparametric test	Mode, frequency, Chi-square test
Ordinal	Equivalence, greater than, less than	Nonparametric test	Median, Spearman rank, Friedman's test, Kendall's tau percentile
Interval	Equivalence, greater than, less than, known ratio of any two intervals	Nonparametric and parametric test	Mean, standard deviation, z -test, t-test, ANOVA, Pearson's r
Ratio	Equivalence, greater than, less than, known ratio of any two ratio	Nonparametric and parametric test	Mean, standard deviation, coefficient of variation, z -test, t-test, ANOVA, Pearson's r

Quantitative variables like nominal and ordinal variables cannot make use of parametric statistical test unlike interval and ratio variables. Interval and ratio levels of measurement can be applied with both the parametric and nonparametric statistical tests. In parametric statistical tests, we can conveniently make use of the mean and standard deviation, the z- test, the t-test, the analysis of variance (ANOVA), and the Chi - square test, the Friedman's test, Kendall's tau, the Binomial test, the Spearman rank correlation, the Kruskall - Wallis test, and Wilcoxon signed rank test, to name a few, to interval and ratio levels of measurements. Interval and ratio measurement can be reduced to nominal or ordinal measurement, while nominal and ordinal measures cannot be upgraded to interval or ratio measures.

Graphic Representation of Data

Graphic representation is another way of analyzing numerical data. A graph is a sort of chart through which statistical data are represented in the form of lines or curves drawn across the coordinated points plotted on its surface. Graphs enable the researcher to study the cause-and-effect relationship between two variables. Graphs help to measure the extent of change in one variable when another variable changes by a certain amount. Graphs also enable us in studying both time series and frequency distribution as they give clear account and precise picture of problem.

Methods to Represent a Frequency Distribution

Generally, four methods are used to represent a frequency distribution graphically. These are Histogram, Smoothed frequency graph and Ogive or Cumulative frequency graph and pie diagram.

1. **Histogram** is a non-cumulative frequency graph; it is drawn on a natural scale in which the representative frequencies of the different class of values are represented through vertical rectangles drawn closed to each other. Measure of central tendency, mode can be easily determined with the help of this graph. **Frequency Polygon** it is a frequency graph which is drawn by joining the coordinating points of the mid-values of the class intervals and their corresponding frequencies.

2. **Smoothed Frequency Polygon.** When the sample is very small, and the frequency distribution is irregular the polygon is very jig-jag. In order to wipe out the irregularities and "also get a better notion of how the figure might look if the data were more numerous, the frequency polygon may be smoothed." In this process to adjust the frequencies we take a series of 'moving' or 'running' averages. To get an adjusted or smoothed frequency we add the frequency of a class interval with the two adjacent intervals, just below and above the class interval. Then the sum is divided by 3. When these adjusted frequencies are plotted against the class intervals on a graph it refers to a smoothed frequency polygon.

3. **Ogive or Cumulative Frequency Polygon.** Ogive is a cumulative frequency graphs drawn on natural scale to determine the values of certain factors like median, Quartile, Percentile etc. In these graphs the exact limits of the class intervals are shown along the X-axis and the cumulative frequen-cies are shown along the Y-axis. Below are given the steps to draw an ogive.

4. **Pie Diagram.** it is a circular statistical graphic, which is divided into slices to illustrate numerical proportion. it is useful when one wants to picture proportions of the total in a striking way. When a population is stratified and each strata is to be presented as a percentage at that time pie diagram is used.

Illustrative Example of Results and Discussion

**CoSIM (Comics cum SIM): An Innovative Material in
Teaching Biology (Samosa, 2021f)**

Results and Discussion

This part present both tabular and textual manner the data gathered from the results of the attitude survey and pretest-posttest of students. The data were treated with appropriate statistical test and were analyzed and interpreted to determine the answers to the questions posed in the study.

Table 2. The students' academic performance before and after the utilization of CoSIM.

	Pretest	Posttest	Gain Score
Mean	19.20	36.43	17.23

Looking at the Table 2, were the students' academic performance before and after the utilization of CoSIM. Taking into account the data provided on the table, it indicates that before the utilization of CoSIM students' academic performance in pretest were 19.20, then in posttest were 36.43. Hence, the students' gain the score of 17.23. More so, it can be concluded that CoSIM had a positive effect on the performance of the students, as evidenced by the significantly greater mean in the posttest than in the pretest. The study confirmed the finding of Anderson et al. (2012) Salviejo et al (2014), Barredo (2014), Dapitan & Caballes (2019), Sinco (2020), that utilization strategic intervention materials in the least-learned competencies in biology improved the students' academic performance. More so, the study supported the findings of Hosler & Boomer, (2012), Da Silva et. al (2016), Casumpang & Enteria (2019), that comics was effective as an instructional material in teaching science concepts.

Table 3. The level of students' attitude in the utilization of CoSIM

	Mean Score	Interpretation
Attitude	4.75	**High Positive Attitude**

The Table 3 established the level of students' attitude in the utilization of CoSIM. Looking forward, the data presented on the table showed that students have high positive attitude in learning biology concepts in photosynthesis based on the mean score 4.75, it indicates that utilization of CoSIM, the students has enjoyed, appreciated, and interested in learning concepts as exposed to intervention materials. It further agrees with different assertions coming from different existing studies of Hosler & Boomer (2012), Affeldt et al. (2018), and Casumpang & Enteria (2019), comics was effective as an instructional material in promoting positive learning attitude towards science concepts.

Table 4: T-test for pretest and posttest score of students in the utilization of CoSIM

t- test computed value	df	t-test critical value	Probability Level	Decision	Interpretation
16.89	29	2.048	< 0.05	H_o is rejected	Significant

Upon computing the data, it appeared that the t- value is 16.89 was exceeds in the t-critical value of 2.048 at the degree of freedom of 29. The result is significant at $p < 0.05$. Therefore, the null hypothesis is thereby, rejected. Thus, there is significant difference in the pretest and posttest score of students in the utilization of CoSIM. The claim is also supported with the study of Arroio (2011) and Weber, et al. (2013) stating that the use of visual and text format presentation gives comic a potential in getting away from traditional mode of delivering classes with the use of traditional textbook materials.

Table 5: Test of Relationship between students' academic performance and students' attitude in the utilization of CoSIM

Pearson r	Relationship	Degree of freedom	t- test computed value	t-test critical value	Probability Level	Decision	Inte
.76	High relationship	28	6.06	2.048	< 0.05	H_o is rejected	Sig

The data revealed the obtained pearson r value is .76 which denotes high positive relationship. This means the higher the academic performance, the higher is the level of students' attitude toward utilization of CoSIM. Since the t- value, 6.06 is greater than the t- critical value, 2.048 at 0.05 and degree of freedom of 28, giving the researcher reasons to reject the null hypothesis in favor of researcher hypothesis. This may be safely concluded that students' academic performance significantly related to the students' attitude toward the utilization of CoSIM in teaching biology particularly in the concepts of photosynthesis.

Assessment Tasks

I. **Direction:** Identify what is being described in the following statements.
   1. This phase involves generating succinct labels (codes) that identify important features of the data that might be relevant to answering the research question.
   2. It is evaluation of the co-occurrence of explicit concepts in the text.
   3. A non-parametric method for testing equality of population medians among groups, using a one-way analysis of variance by ranks.
   4. it is drawn on a natural scale in which the representative frequencies of the different class of values are represented through vertical rectangles drawn closed to each other.
   5. Statistical treatment used to assess whether the means of two groups are statistically different from each other.
   6. It is drawing a conclusions from data using statistical tests.
   7. It calculates and compares the differences between each set of pairs and analyses the list of differences.
   8. In this phase, themes are typically refined, which sometimes involves them being split, combined, or discarded.
   9. This is the most versatile among the test of statistical significance, as can be both as a test of relationship or test of difference.
   10. A graphic representation used when a population is stratified and each strata is to be presented as a percentage.

II. **Direction:** Identify the following statistical treatment either Nonparametric or parametric.
   1. Standard deviation
   2. One sample Z-test
   3. One sample Wilcoxon signed rank test.
   4. Kruskal-Wallis H test
   5. Mean
   6. Spearman rank correlation coefficient
   7. Mann Whitney U test
   8. One-way ANOVA
   9. Independent samples t-test
   10. Interquartile range

Performance Tasks

Design and Make Results and Discussion

Looking your collected data from the survey questionnaire or interview, tally each of the responses of your participants/respondents by following the basic principles of quantitative procedure or qualitative procedure for thematic/content analysis. Show your findings in tables and interpret each of the findings with supported literature and studies.

Rubric for Writing the Results and Discussion

Criteria	Excellent 15-20	Good 8-14	Poor 1-7
Introduction	Use all of the titles of subsection in the introduction as sign posts for the reader to know what is coming.	Preview the contents of the chapter. Explain what organization of the data and analysis using themes provided from design, instrument or analysis and align with the research question.	Identify problem & restate the research question (do not repeat your whole chapter 1).
Data Presentation	The findings are detailed and flow easily.	Visual representations (form of tables, figures, quotes, or photos) are properly identified, self-descriptive, informative, directly related to and referred to within the narrative of text, and immediately adjacent comments are provided.	Describe the findings within context of the setting, questions and field of education.
Data Analysis	Sufficient evidence is provided. Sophisticated explanation and integration of research in the field.	Iterative use a systematic review, make sure nothing is left out of analysis.	Appropriately analyze and explain your analysis.
Interpretation	Articulate how author's insider/outsider impacted the findings and interpretations. Articulate insight gained from the study in reference to data analysis	Intelligently interpret using layman approach to explaining contextualized data – so that anyone can understand findings and their value to the field. Include inconsistent findings and discuss possible alternative interpretation.	Interpret how you made sense of the findings outcomes are logically and systematically summarized and interpret in relation to their importance to the research questions.
Summary	Provide a transition to chapter 5	Re-articulate research question	Summarize key concepts in chapter 4

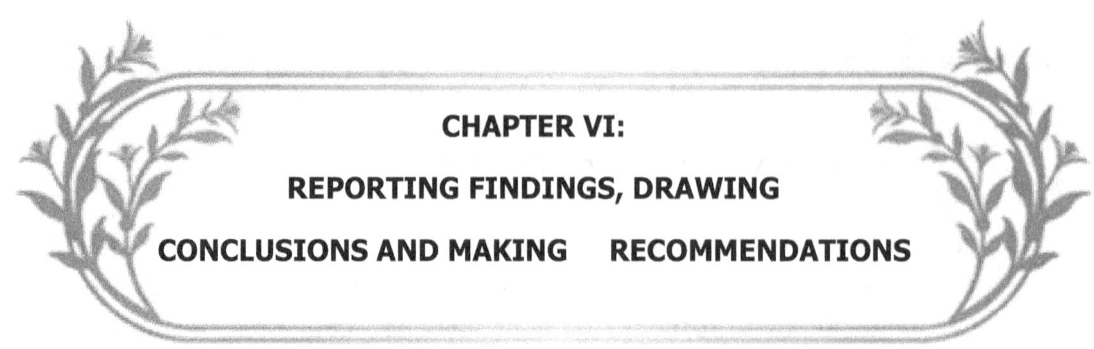

CHAPTER VI:

REPORTING FINDINGS, DRAWING

CONCLUSIONS AND MAKING   RECOMMENDATIONS

LEARNING OBJECTIVES

At the end of this chapter, students should be able to

1. forms logical conclusions.
2. makes recommendations based on conclusions.
3. writes and presents clear report

After the collection of data and collating, presenting, analyzing, interpreting, and discussing the results, the formulation of concluding part of the research follows. The concluding part is composed of the summary of finding, conclusion, and recommendation.

Summary of Findings

The summary of findings puts together the highlight of the important findings of the study. It is a condensation of the steps taken by the researcher and the subsequent findings. In a very concise manner, the researcher restates the problems, the methods used, techniques and tools utilized in gathering and interpreting the data and then, he states the answers to the questions as stated in Chapter 1.

In summarizing the findings of the study, specific problems are restated one at a time and these followed by the highlight of the results of the investigation. The summary of findings serves as an overview or a resume of the most important findings of the entire inquiry.

If there are only two specific answers or findings in chapter IV, there should only two results/findings summarized in this section. Tables, graph and other figures of presentation are excluded here. Important results are stated as concisely and as directly as possible.

Ariola (2006), suggested the following guidelines in writing summary of findings.

1. Enumeration of findings should follow the sequence of the subproblems of the study.
2. Only important major findings should be highlighted.

3. Findings should be stated as cautiously as possible without further discussion.
4. The findings must be consistent with the analysis of data.
5. No new data should be introduced into the findings if they are not found in the analysis of data, or not part of the study.

Conclusions

The conclusion (s) is an abstraction drawn from the findings of the study and is tied to the questions investigated (Ochave et. al, 1992). Conclusion should be consistent with and must drawn from the findings. If there are only two summarized results, there must also be conclusions. Conclusions should be arranged in accordance with the presentation and arrangement of the findings. Rejection or acceptance of the hypothesis (es) are explained briefly in this section. Conclusion should be stated briefly and in straight forward manner so that reader can remember it easily, it is important that every problem raised , a conclusion is reached by the researcher.

Rebustes (2002) identifies the following guidelines in writing conclusions.

1. Conclusions are inferences, deductions, abstractions, implications, interpretation, general statements, and or generalizations based upon the findings. Conclusions are the logical and valid outgrowth of the findings. They should not contain any numerals because numerals generally limit the forceful effect or impact and scope of the generalization. No conclusion be made that are not based upon the findings.

2. Conclusions should appropriately answer the specific questions raised at the beginning of the investigation in the order they are given under the statement of the problem. The study becomes almost meaningless if the questions raised are not properly answered by the conclusions.

3. Conclusion should point out what were factually learned from the inquiry. However, no conclusion should be drawn from the implied or indirect effects of the findings.

4. Conclusions should be formulated concisely, that is, brief and short, yet the convey all the necessary information resulting from the study as required by the specific questions.

5. Without any strong evidence to the contrary, conclusion should be stated categorically. They should be worded as if they are 100 percent true and correct. They should not give any hint that the researchers have some doubts about their validity and reliability. The use of

qualifiers such as probably, perhaps, may be and the like should be avoided as much as possible.

6. Conclusions should refer only to the population, area, or subject of the study.

7. Conclusions should not be repetitions of any statements anywhere in the thesis. They may be recapitulations, if necessary, but they should be worded differently, and they should convey the same information as the statement recapitulated.

Recommendations

Recommendation are suggestions for the improvement of the existing policies, practices, program or prevailing conditions under study. The main goal of research is the betterment and or improvement of life and this goal should be the focal point in writing the recommendations.

Recommendations should be derived from the data gathered and from the conclusion drawn from the findings. Its common practice to enumerate the recommendations and number them and to identify specific person, institutions, or sections to whom the recommendations are addressed.

Barrot (2017) suggested the following guidelines in writing recommendations.

1. Make sure that your recommendation are in accordance with the conclusion and limitation of your study. Furthermore, align your recommendation with the purpose and scope of your research.

2. Make your recommendation as specific as possible for them to become workable and practical.

3. Write your recommendations concisely and clearly. This will help the readers immediately recognize the impact of your study.

4. As much as possible, refrain from offering recommendations that could have been easily addressed as you were conducting your study. Otherwise, these might be construed only as an after -thought.

Illustrative Example 1 of Conclusion & Recommendation.

Effectiveness of Claim, Evidence, and Reasoning as an Innovation to Develop Students' Scientific Argumentative Writing Skills (Samosa, 2020b)

Conclusions.

The research results of and discussion on the effectiveness of CER as innovation to develop students' scientific argumentative writing skills in Biology teaching draw several conclusions.

1. The students' scientific argumentative writing skills in biology learning after the CER framework application is found at the proficient in writing the claim, proficient in writing evidence and excelling in writing the reasoning. This research has implied that CER as innovation are effectively increased the components of writing the claim, evidence, and reasoning in biology teaching.
2. The students have high positive attitude based on the five indicators toward nature of science after the CER framework application.
3. After the CER framework application, the students improved their appreciation in learning of science into positive attitude.
4. It is evident that after the CER, students' appreciation in scientific writing improved into positive attitude.
5. The students have high positive attitude based on the five indicators toward thinking and learning science after the CER framework application.
6. After the students are very comfortable in using CER as innovation to develop students' scientific argumentative writing skills.
7. The implementation of CER results is the significant improvement on students' scientific argumentative writing skills in biology teaching after the experiment
8. Claim, Evidence and Reasoning increases students' ability to identify, critique, and compare the quality of evidence in written arguments.
9. Participation in argumentative writing exercises helps to strengthen Students' scientific claims.
10. Students need continuous feedback in order to improve and to think- like- a scientist.

Recommendations.

Based on the findings of the study and the conclusion drawn, the following are recommended:

1. Further research is needed on possible connections between argumentative writing instruction in the science curriculum and the language arts curriculum, and how teachers can potentially collaborate and/or design curriculum to support this practice among the different content areas.
2. Utilize the used of the CER Framework in teaching science subjects for further research with bigger population.
3. Conduct a School – Based workshop on proper implementation of the CER as innovation to develop students' scientific argumentative writing skills.
4. For more comprehensive findings, further studies on the same area of concentration may be conducted for improving science education where the students will be benefited.

**Cultivating Research Culture: Capacity Building Program Toward
Initiatives to Improve Teachers Self-Efficacy , Research Anxiety
and Research Attitude (Samosa, 2021d)**

Conclusion.
Based on the findings of the study, the following conclusion are drawn.
1. Most of the teacher respondent are Technology Livelihood Education Teachers with a 6 – 10 years of teaching in the public school and bachelor's degree holder.
2. Teachers' respondents have high research self-efficacy.
3. Teachers have high positive towards on the conduct of action research.
4. Teachers have high positive attitude on the conduct of action research.
5. Teacher respondents described the capacity building program towards research initiative in conducting action research as highly effective.
6. There is significant relationship between research self-efficacy, research anxiety, and research attitude towards research initiative in conducting action research and the profile of novice teachers – researchers.
7. There is significant difference in the assessment of capacity building program for action research when novice teachers – researchers group according to profile.
8. There is significant relationship in the research self-efficacy, research anxiety and research attitude among novice teachers – researchers.
9. The Level of the Research Culture Index of Graceville National High School were fair which the scored below 80% in the research culture index.

Recommendation
The following are some significant management implications drawn from the findings of the study.
1. This study, therefore, provides an implication that there is a need for the Schools Division of San Jose del Monte City to adapt these capacity building program in the division level to help the teachers raise their level of capability in research. Such program may include not only a series of training focusing not only on increasing the teachers' knowledge, attitude and lessening their anxiety in research but at the same time conducting, presenting, and publishing their research output. Further, the SDO San Jose del Monte City may intensify the conduct of mentoring and training to produce quality research and craft a functional teachers' development plan for advanced education for broadening their knowledge and research skills.
2. The officials of the Department of Education may provide public school teachers with the needed motivation to research by providing them monetary and non-monetary incentives and adequate management support to polish their research skills, attitude, and capability in disseminating and publishing the results in different media.
3. The Teachers should continue upgrading their educational attainment by attending graduate and postgraduate education in the area of specialization, and by attending research-related conferences.
4. The research capability training program consisting of various levels from lectures, hands-on workshop, and writing research articles for colloquium and possible publication should be fully implemented immediately and regularly monitor its effectiveness.

List the References

The reference list complies all the bibliographic information for the materials you used in preparing your research. Providing a reference list aids your readers in tracing the works that guided you in conducting your study, thus making your research more reliable. It also helps you avoid committing intellectual dishonesty since a reference list is proof that you acknowledge other studies that shapes your own.

Below are some guidelines you can follow in listing your references (Barrot, 2017b).

1. **Make sure that your reference list contains all of the works and publication you used for your research**. All the references that you cited in the text itself must be included in your reference list.

2. **Cite your sources completely**. Aside from providing the name of the references itself, you need to cite the author of the work; the publisher of the material (if it is printed); the date of its publication or release; and the date that you retrieved it (if it is an online reference).

3. **Exercise consistency in the format of your bibliographical entries**. Strictly follow the format for citing your references according to the citation style you are using in your research (APA,MLA, or Chicago). The citation style you are using will also determine the title or heading of your reference list. Paper written in the APA style use heading "Reference", the MLA Style uses the heading "Works Cited," and the Chicago style uses the heading "Bibliography."

4. **Take note of other consideration in citing your references.** For instance, make sure to arrange your references alphabetically. In addition, use en dash (–) instead of hyphen (-) when presenting range (e.g., 5 – 13)

Illustrative Example of Reference

Cooperative Learning Approach as Innovation to Improve Students' Academic Achievement and Attitude in Teaching Biology (Samosa, 2021e)

References

Ajaja, O. P., & Eravwoke, O. U. (2010). Effects of cooperative learning strategy on junior secondary school students achievement in integrated science. *The Electronic Journal for Research in Science & Mathematics Education, 14*(1).

Akhtar, K., Perveen, Q., Kiran, S., Rashid, M., & Satti, A. K. (2012). A study of student's attitudes towards cooperative learning. *International Journal of Humanities and Social Science, 2*(11), 141-147.

Hossain, A., & Tarmizi, R. A. (2013). Effects of cooperative learning on students' achievement and attitudes in secondary mathematics. *Procedia-Social and Behavioral Sciences, 93*, 473-477.

Bukunola, BA J & Idowu, O D. (2012). Effectiveness of Cooperative Learning Strategies on Nigerian Junior Secondary Students' Academic Achievement in Basic Science. *British Journal of Education, Society & Behavioural Science, 2*(3), 307-325.

Farzaneh, N., & Nejadansari, D. (2014). Students' Attitude towards Using Cooperative Learning for Teaching Reading Comprehension. *Theory & Practice in Language Studies, 4*(2).

Mehta, S & Kulshrestha, A K. (2014). Implementation of Cooperative Learning in Science: A Developmental-cum-Experimental Study. *Education Research International.* https://doi.org/10.1155/2014/431542 .

Montebon, D. T. (2014). K12 science program in the Philippines: Student perception on its implementation. *International Journal of Education and Research, 2*(12), 153-164.

Muraya, D. N., & Kimamo, G. (2011). Effects of cooperative learning approach on biology mean achievement scores of secondary school students in Machakos District, Kenya. *Educational Research and Reviews, 6*(12), 726-745.

Nnorom, N. R. (2015). Effect of cooperative learning instructional strategy on senior secondary school students achievement in biology in anambra state, Nigeria. *International Journal for Cross-Disciplinary Subjects in Education, 5*(1), 2424-2427.

Sani, U. T. (2015). Effects of cooperative learning strategy on senior secondary school students' performance in quantitative chemistry in Kebbi state, Nigeria. *Journal of Education and Social Sciences, 1*, 30-35.

Tran, V. D. (2014). The effects of cooperative learning on the academic achievement and knowledge retention. *International journal of higher education, 3*(2), 131-140

Assessment Tasks

Direction: Write T if the statement is true and F if false.
1. The summary may contain personal comments from the researcher.
2. The summary contains inferences from the findings.
3. The summary of findings may contain an actual response from the respondents in a form of direct quotations.
4. New information may be injected into the summary.
5. The coverage of the summary of findings depends on the number of research questions or objectives.
6. At least one of your conclusions should directly address your general research problems.
7. Assumptions that are not supported by data can be included in the conclusion.
8. Your conclusion should be extended to other contexts and wider population.
9. Each conclusion should correspond to one item in the findings.
10. The practical implications of the findings are an integral part of the conclusion.
11. Your paper should provide recommendation for future research.
12. Your recommendation should align with the conclusions.
13. The recommendation should be as specific as possible.

14. Providing reference list makes your study more reliable.
15. In -text citation is where all of the references used in the study are compiled.

Performance Tasks.

Design and Make Summary of Finding, Conclusion, Recommendation and Reference List

1. Write your summary of finding based on the sequences from your research question or research objectives.
2. Write the conclusion of your study based on the sequences from your research question or research objectives.
3. Write the recommendation of your study Use the following guide questions.
   a) What can you recommend to future researchers to prevent the occurrence of negative results in the study?
   b) What can you recommend as new or additional courses of actions to improve or to make more effective program or policies?
   c) What possible areas of research within the topic can be studied further by future researchers who are interested to study the same topic?
4. Make the reference list for your research paper. follow the correct format and citation style.

Rubric for Writing the Summary of Finding, Conclusion, Recommendation and Reference List

Criteria	Excellent 16-20	Very Good 11-15	Good 6-10	Needs Improvement 1-5
Major Findings and Results of the Study	All data are recorded and organized in clear manner. All visible observations are provided. Complete and correct analysis of data is provided.	All data are recorded and organized in a clear manner. All visible observations are provided. Analysis of data is provided with a few errors.	All data are recorded and organized in a clear manner. Visible observations are missing. Analysis of data is provided with a few errors.	Incorrect data are provided regardless of inclusion or presentation of all other criteria.
Conclusion	Explains the research problem very clearly and how the study	Explains the research problem fairly well and how the study adds	Does not explain the research problem clearly and how the	Conclusion is very unclear.

	adds new understanding or fills up an important gap in the literature; explains very clearly how the research contributes to new knowledge or how it provides a new understanding or interpretation of the research problem.	new understanding or fills up an important gap in the literature; explains fairly well how the research contributes to new knowledge or how it provides a new understanding or interpretation of the research problem.	study adds new understanding or fills up an important gap in the literature; does not explain clearly how the research contributes to new knowledge or how it provides a new understanding or interpretation of the research problem.	
Recommendations of the study	Explain the weaknesses and shortfalls of the research very clearly; clearly provide new or additional courses of action to improve the research or to make it more effective.	Explain the weakness and shortfalls of the research fairly well; provide some new or additional courses of actions to improve the research or to make it more effective.	Do not explain the weaknesses and shortfalls of the research clearly. Do not provide any new or additional course of action to improve the research or to make it more effective.	Recommendations were very unclear.
Reference	Done in the correct format wit no errors.	Done in the correct format with few errors.	Done in the correct format with some errors.	Done in the correct format with many errors.

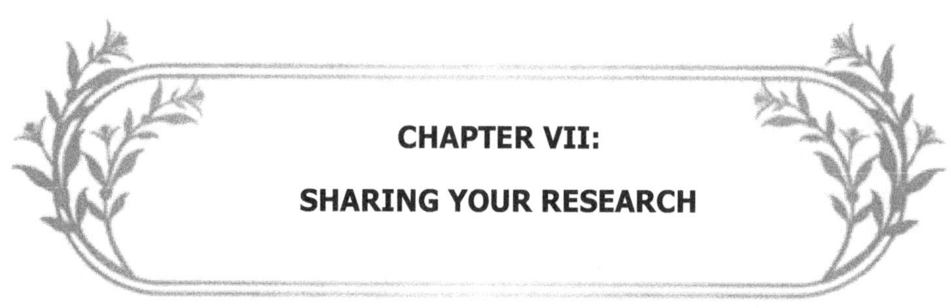

LEARNING OBJECTIVES

At the end of this chapter, students should be able to

1. defends written research report;
2. revises written research report based on suggestions and recommendations of panelists;
3. submits final written research report

Research Report

One of the reasons for carrying out research is to add to the existing body of knowledge. Therefore, when conducting research, you need to document your processes and findings in a research report. With a research report, it is easy to outline the findings of your systematic investigation and any gaps needing further inquiry. Knowing how to create a detailed research report will prove useful when you need to conduct research.

A **research report** is a well-crafted document that outlines the processes, data, and findings of a systematic investigation. It is an important document that serves as a first-hand account of the research process, and it is typically considered as an objective and accurate source of information.

In many ways, a research report can be considered as a summary of the research process that clearly highlights findings, recommendations, and other important details. Reading a well-written research report should provide you with all the information you need about the core areas of the research process.

Features of a Research Report

So how do you recognize a research report when you see one? Here are some of the basic features that define a research report.

1. it is a detailed presentation of research processes and findings, and it usually includes tables and graphs.

2. It is written in a formal language.

3. A research report is usually written in the third person.

4. It is informative and based on first-hand verifiable information.

5. It is formally structured with headings, sections, and bullet points.

6. It always includes recommendations for future actions.

The Thesis Proposal

In general, the first three chapters of your proposal are the Introduction, Literature Review and Methodology. Take note of the following verb tenses when writing your chapters:

Introduction	Chapter 1	Simple present and future tense
Literature Review	Chapter 2	Present but mostly past
Methodology	Chapter 3	Present but mostly future

Your research adviser is your ally. In order to obtain enough support from your research adviser and your thesis committee members, you have to show that you have done your work well; therefore, you need to be prepared before a proposal meeting. It can take several meetings before you are ready to defend your proposal. Thesis research is directed research. Your research adviser must give you advice, and you must do the work. When your proposal is approved, the process of operationalizing your method(s) to find answers to your questions begins. When it is finished, the process of rewriting the proposal can also start.

Introduction

The first chapter of a proposal consists of several subheadings or sections: background, research questions, objectives, limitations, rationale, hypothesis (optional), statement of the problem, and methodology. Discuss with your adviser as to which section should be omitted or added.

Subheadings and what they mean:
- **Background** – What is the context of this problem? In what situation or environment can it be observed? (Provide sufficient information for the readers to understand the topic you are researching about.)

- **Statement of the Problem** – What is it that we do not know? What is the gap in our knowledge this research will fill? What needs to be improved?

- **Research Questions** – What is it that you want to find out? (a question that's broad enough to stimulate your interest and narrow enough that you can provide a convincing answer)

- ***Hypotheses** – What ideas are suggested as possible explanation for the problem, situation or condition and will be proved to be correct or incorrect by the research?

- ***Scope of the Study** – Is the study limited to a specific geographical area or people, or to only certain aspects of the situation? Is there any aspect of the problem the researcher will not discuss?

- **Limitation of the Study** – Is there any factor, condition or circumstances that will prevent the researcher from achieving all his/her objectives?

- **Theoretical - Conceptual Framework** – presents your ideas in a model or illustration of what you intend to investigate, and some theories related to it. The research problem is a part of the conceptual framework that you will build based on the existing theories and research.

** The sections, Scope of the Study and Limitation of the Study, can be combined in one section to form the "Scope and Limitation of the Study". When writing the remaining chapters of the thesis, the Limitation of the Study should be included in Chapter 3 as part of the Methodology.*
**Some proposals do not need hypotheses.*

Below are some suggested steps for writing the first chapter or Introduction.

1. Think of topics that interest you. Discuss your topics with your adviser before choosing the most interesting and practical one.
2. You have to search for more information first in order to understand what has been studied about the subject or your topic of interest.
3. Define a research problem.
4. Before you can formulate or define the appropriate research questions, you need to be familiar with your topic and current trends/research advances on the topic. A pilot study or feasibility study can be done before the actual research process.
5. Research questions should be developed keeping in mind time constraints—can these be answered by only one study or several studies?

Usually in qualitative approaches, research questions are formulated, instead of a hypothesis/hypotheses. Qualitative research starts an investigation with a concept.

Quantitative research approaches use the hypothesis as the frame for the methodology. Here, you will have an appropriate framework and variables considered.

In both approaches, the main research question is the basis for the hypotheses and objectives of the research.

6. Hypotheses can be developed from the research questions. Designing a hypothesis is supported by a good research question and will influence the type of research design for the study.
7. The development of the research objective can be done after the development of the research questions or hypothesis.
8. Do not forget to CITE current or relevant work of other authors and try to use the different techniques in incorporating other authors' ideas in your writing, summarizing, paraphrasing and directly quoting the source. This should be applied all throughout your paper. See Citations and References – The APA Style Guide for a guide to acknowledging the works of other authors when incorporating their ideas into your writing.

The Literature Review

In this chapter (and in the succeeding chapters of your thesis or dissertation), you need to write an introductory paragraph or paragraphs that show the following:
1. what the topic is about;
2. the research or theoretical framework;
3. reasons for reviewing the literature (show the gap and how this research would fill that gap)
4. what is discussed in the chapter, the order or sequence of the review;
5. what is included and not included in the chapter.

The second part is the Body. The following are some elements that can be included in the second part of the Literature Review chapter. Discuss with your adviser to finalize the sections and sub-headings.
1. a general view of the literature being reviewed to the specific focus of your research.
2. the relationship between your chosen topic and the wider subject area; for instance, between obesity in children and obesity in general; between perspectives of risks in communities and disaster resilience.
3. organization of the literature according to sub-topics or common themes:
   a) historical background
   b) methodologies/ hypotheses/ models
   c) popular views vs. other views (similar and contrasting views)
   d) major questions presented.
   e) general conclusions made by the authors.
4. an in-depth examination of the literature in each sub-topic or theme presented (#3)

The last part is the Chapter Summary.
1. Summarize the important aspects of the existing body of literature.

2. Assess the current state of the literature reviewed.

Methodology

This chapter presents your *research design* which describes and justifies the methods that will be used to collect your data. It should be well-developed in order to obtain all the information required to answer your research questions, test a theory, or explain a situation relevant to the main aim of the research.

Start this chapter with a short introduction to your research design. In this section, the research questions, hypotheses, and objectives must be presented. An overview of the research approach, and the techniques and measurements that will be used to analyze data are also included in the introduction.

The next part of this chapter, or the Body, consists of some or all sections shown below. Each section should be described and explained in detail. Discuss with your adviser for additional sections and sub-headings for each section or a more appropriate structure.

1. Research design
2. Respondents of the Study
3. Sampling Design & Techniques
4. Data Gathering Procedure
5. Statistical Treatment

The Final Chapters of Thesis

At this stage, you have already collected as much data as you can and are ready to process and analyze such a huge amount of information. However, expect a lot of changes in your process, methods, and chapters. These changes can come from your research adviser, too.

The first step you need to do is to revisit the first three chapters of your thesis. Here, you would need to make the necessary corrections to some of the sections presented during the proposal stage. For example, you might have to fine-tune your research questions and objectives based on the data you have gathered or what you have found during the research process. The Scope and Limitations of the Study section in Chapter 1 would now have to be included in Chapter 3. Another section, Organization of the Study, must be added in Chapter 1. Check the figure below for the main parts of a thesis.

Main Parts of a thesis or dissertation

Components	Chapter	Verb Tense
Title page		
Acknowledgments		simple present and past
Abstract		simple present and past
Table of Contents		
Table of Contents		
List of Abbreviations		
List of Tables and Figures		
Introduction	Chapter I	simple present and past
Literature Review	Chapter II	present but mostly past
Methodology	Chapter III	mostly simple past
Results and Discussion	Chapter IV	simple present, past and present perfect
Summary of Finding , Conclusion and Recommendations	Chapter V	simple present and present perfect
References	Follow the APA style guides.	
Appendices		

Results and Discussions

If this chapter is generally brief, presenting the results, and explaining and interpreting them can be combined in one chapter. Otherwise, the Results and Discussion section should be in separate or defined sections or chapters. Start with a brief introduction of this chapter.

Results: answers to the research questions which are generated from the collected data. In this section, evidence is presented through graphical and/or textual form organized in sub-sections. Your opinion should not be included when presenting the results.

Descriptive or frequency statistical results of all variables must be reported first before specific statistical tests (e.g., regression analysis). For instance, the profile of participants or respondents, or characteristics of the sample is presented first if available. Results from a *regression and/or correlation analysis* are presented after all the descriptive and frequencies for all variables, or summaries of the data set have been presented.

Specific quotes from interviews must be presented under a specific theme or sub-theme in the same way results from focus group discussions are reported. When reporting results from observations, present the conversation, behavior, or condition you have noticed first. Then, write your comments.

Discussion: explains the meaning of the results presented in specific sections and links them to previous research studies. It explains why the findings are weak, strong, or significant, and their limitations. A further review of the literature might be required to enhance the discussion of results.

Summary of Finding, Conclusion and Recommendations

Introduce this chapter. First, refer back to the problem or topic that you have presented in Chapter 1 and what you hoped to achieve at the beginning of the research. The research questions you tried to answer must also be reviewed in this chapter as well as your hypotheses, if applicable. It is important to also reexamine the methodology followed in the research and show how the objectives were achieved (or were not achieved) with the application of different methods and techniques.

There are six possible components can be included in the concluding chapter of quantitative dissertations: "statement of hypothesis (or purpose), summary of main points / findings (whether they support the hypothesis; whether they align with, or differ from, other researchers' findings), possible explanations for the findings and/or speculations about them, limitations of the study, implications of your findings, recommendations for future research, action or policy changes, and practical applications."

Abstract

When all the chapters have been finalized, you are now ready to prepare the abstract. It is written in the form of a summary, briefly describing the research problem, the aims of the research, the methods used to achieve them, and the main findings and conclusions. Although the abstract is very short (approximately 1-2 paragraphs), it can be considered as the most significant part of your thesis or dissertation. The abstract provides a general impression of what your research is about and allows other researchers to have a broad understanding of your work. When applying for conferences, your abstract is assessed by an organizing committee for relevance and quality. Make sure to create an impact—write an impressive abstract.

Common Mistakes in Research and How to Address them (Trinidad, 2019b)

Research Process Mistakes

Mistakes	Remedies
1. **Unclear purpose and audience**	Clarify why you are writing the research (knowledge production, policy analysis, etc.).
	Keep in mind who you are writing for (general audience vs. specific experts in the field).
2. **Procrastination**	Try to manage your time well and chuck tasks.
	Be mindful of your scripts and delaying tactics.
	Create a matrix of activities in terms of urgency and importance.
3. **Neglecting guidelines, rubrics, and instructions**	Check the journal or department's instructions for writers, including spelling, word limit, citation style, and paper structure.
4. **Infeasibility of research**	Check ahead of time if you will be permitted by the institution, administrators, or officials to conduct your research.
	Discern if you have enough time to finish your research.
	Try doing pilot studies, survey, or interviews with a smaller scale before going for a bigger scale.
5. **Group conflicts**	Manage each other's expectations and working styles from the start.
	Talk about how you plan to get feedback on your work.
	Beware of gift and ghost authorship.
6. **Personal problems and emergencies**	If there is a risk that a personal problem may occur during the conduct of your research, think in advance how can address it.
	If the problem happens, tell your research adviser or groupmates about your situation.

Research Conceptualization

Mistakes	Remedies
1. **Lack of preliminary reading**	Read and reflect about the topic you wish to pursue.
	Get exposed to studies, both classic and recent.
2. **Vague research questions**	Be careful about having questions that are either too broad or too specific.
	Think questions that are grounded in a particular reality and phenomenon.
	Avoid questions that are loaded with many assumptions.
	Be open to how your research question can change in the process of research.
3. **Unidentified research gap**	Think about how your research adds to our current knowledge or what new insights you plan to say.

	Avoid research topics that have been studied to death.
4. Unidentified hypotheses or argument	Write a hypothesis that can be tested with the variables you have at your disposal.
	Write a tentative argument that clearly answers the research questions.
5. Unaligned questions and argument.	You have the choice of either changing your argument or changing your research questions.
6. Unclear research structure	Be familiar with the IMRAD model followed by most research in the natural, physical, and social sciences.
	Most research usually have sections on introduction, methods, results, and discussion.
7. Undefined terms	Write out acronyms during the first time they appear.
	Define scientific and technical terms during the first time they appear.
	Operationalize concepts such that they can be quantified or qualified.
8. Literature review as book or article summaries	Note that the literature review expresses your stance on a topic and need not be summaries of things you have read.
	Literature reviews can challenge previous research or provide a bird's eye – view of the topic.
9. Incoherent Literature	Create a structure for your literature review. This can take the form of topical arrangement, compare-and-contrast, advantages-and-disadvantages, chronological arrangement, factors, problem-and-solution structure.
10. Outdated or unreliable literature	Find up-to-date research, findings, and examples.
	Search in more reliable or scholarly search engines like Jstor, EBSCOHost, Google Books, Google Scholar.
11. Unclear differentiation between framework and literature review.	Although both help researchers conceptualize the study and identify research gaps, a literature review does not need a conceptual map but a framework should provide a structure of how ideas are connected with each other.

Research Methods

Mistakes	Remedies
1. Inappropriate research methods	Clarify whether you will use a qualitative, quantitative, or mixed methods approach.
	Think of a plan or strategy with how you will answer your research question.
	Reflect if the answer you obtain through your methods is the answer to your main research question.
2. Sampling mistakes	Distinguish whether you are doing probability or non-probability sampling.
	Be familiar with possible sources of bias with your data.

	Clarify what will make participants be included or excluded from your research.
3. **Erroneous survey questionnaires**	When creating your own tests, beware of common pitfalls and issue on confidentiality, inaccurate choices, different ranges, types of questions (and responses), using Likert scales, and having open – and closed – ended questions.
4. **Interview and FGD mistakes**	Use an interview when you want to get in-depth information or confidential narratives.
	Use FGD when looking at social interactions and differences in perspectives.
	Provide information about your research to your participants.
	Give your participants time to prepare for the interview and send a formal invitation to let them know what will be asked of them.
	When doing the interview itself, have a coherent structure and come prepared with possible follow -up questions.
5. **Untranscribed or uncoded data**	Bring a recording device to record your informants' answer.
	Transcribe the interviews faithfully.
	Systematically code your interviews to see common themes and answers.
6. **Unaddressed ethical concerns**	If necessary, seek research ethics approval for your study.
	Clarify if you will be involving vulnerable populations in your research.
	Ensure confidentially and privacy of your participants.
	Treat participants with respect and dignity.
7. **Inability to foresee and disclose risks.**	Inform your research participants about the possible physical, psychological, social and legal risks that come with joining the research (if there are any).
	Come prepared with plans to minimize the risk or how to address the problems when they happen.
8. **Inability to obtain informed consent**	Your letters to participants should include the purpose of your study, procedure and duration of involvement, potential risks and benefits, statement of voluntary participation and right to withdraw, ensuring confidentiality of data, asking permission for recording, compensation, and contact information.
9. **Unclear methods discussion.**	Discuss the participants and how they were recruited.
	Clarify dependent, independent, and control variables.
	Show how you plan to do data or statistical analyses, or visualizations.
	Show how you analyzed your qualitative data through coding and searching for themes.
10. **Difficult to find resources**	See where you can obtain access to achieved documents.
	Look at the available sources first before proceeding to the research paper.

Mistakes	Remedies
1. **Inappropriate research methods**	Do not input your own data, write observations, or interview that did not happen, selectively submit results, or hide negative findings.
	Always verify information you write in your research.
2. **Incorrect figures**	Note the difference between doing bar graphs, histogram, pie graphs, and other data visualization techniques.
	Beware of figures without titles, labels, clear sources, and with no focus.
3. **Incorrect tables**	Distinguish tables for descriptive statistics, frequency, correlations, and regressions.
	Write the statistical significance (e.g. ** *$p < 0.001$)
	Order and group similar variables.
4. **Absent or unrelated data explanation.**	Describe which part of the tables the reader should focus on .
	Organize your results section according to the progression of the tables.
5. **Incorrect use of quotes.**	Beware of having too many few quotes.
	Clarify whether you are using a block quotes or a regular quotes.
	Talk about themes and supplement them with quotes or narratives.
	You may paraphrase or summarize long quotes.
6. **Non -identified informants**	For qualitative research, identify your research participant or informant.
	Provide information about background characteristics that may affect their answers.
	Some participants may be identified by name because of their expertise or position.
7. **Plagiarism**	Beware of the different types of plagiarism.
	If it is a verbatim quote, put it in quotation.
	Cite the sources of your ideas or information.
	Paraphrase accurately in your own words.
8. **Absent or unclear discussion section**	Remind the reader about the question and argument.
	Synthesize findings and deeper meanings.
	Connect results to broader insights.
	Note unexpected findings and alternative explanation.
9. **Inability to engage counterargument**	Provide a space to share opposing opinions.
	You can refute these counterarguments in your research
	Be careful with having too many twists and turns in you research.
10. **Research question remains unanswered.**	Go back to your research question and reflect on whether you were able to answer it, or whether the research was consistent with your original question.

Writing

Mistakes	Remedies
1. Informal tone and language	Be consistent with the use of the first person or third person pronouns.
	If you use pronouns, do so sparingly.
	Avoid words that are obligating, direct, inaccurate, or exaggerated.
2. Unclear point	Use the point index to clarify your thesis statement.
	Try to underline the main point for every paragraph and see if there is coherence among paragraphs.
3. Unconnected paragraph	Use transition expressions (like accordingly, despite this, although, as a matter of fact...).
	Be conscious oof how your old information interacts with your new information.
	Outline broad ideas and show the next sentences or paragraphs are connected.
4. Mistakes with sentences	Keep the subject and verb close to each other.
	Know which common tenses are used for research.
	Always check whether the sentences express a complete thought.
	Identify the modifier and see if the word closest the word is it truly modifier.
	Vary the length and structure of your sentences.
5. Mistakes with words.	Avoid contractions, abbreviations, and acronyms (that have not been defined).
	Go for concise writing rather than worldly writing.
	Be careful with interchangeable and technical words.
6. Mistakes with italics, bold, and underline	Use italics for light emphasis and bold for heavy emphasis.
	Use italics for book titles, journal titles, cinematics productions, television programs, and artwork.
	In addition, use italics also foreign words, scientific names, and some statistical notations.
7. Mistakes in punctuation	Semicolons are used to join two complete ideas.
	Colons are used to introduce a list, show emphasis, or introduce a quotes.
	Dashes are used to create a break in the structure of the sentence.
	Parentheses are for added clarification.
	Quotation marks are used for repeating quotes verbatim or short articles.
	Apostrophes are used to show possession.
8. Mistakes in footnotes	Check whether you have all the correct details.
	Refers to the formatting guide.
	Use a citation management system.
9. Mistakes with in -text citation	Be familiar with the convention of using parenthetical citations.
	Ensure that you have all cited sources in your bibliography.

Assessment Tasks

I. **Direction:** Identify the parts of research are being described in the following statement.

    1. It answers to the research questions which are generated from the collected data.
    2. it presents your research design which describes and justifies the methods that will be used to collect your data.
    3. It explains the meaning of the results presented in specific sections and links them to previous research studies.
    4. It consists of several subheadings or sections: background, research questions, objectives, limitations, rationale, hypothesis (optional), statement of the problem, and methodology.
    5. It is written in the form of a summary, briefly describing the research problem, the aims of the research, the methods used to achieve them, and the main findings and conclusions.

II. **Direction:** Write T if the statement is true and F if false.

    1. Colons are used to added clarification.
    2. Always check whether the sentences express a complete thought in writing your research.
    3. italics are used for book titles, journal titles, cinematics productions, television programs, and artwork.
    4. The researcher must describe which part of the tables the reader should focus on.
    5. Cite the sources of your ideas or information.

Oral Presentation & Research Report

Direction: Write and submit the draft of your research report and present orally. Your Output will be assessed using the following rubrics below.

Rubric for Writing the Research Report

Criteria	Excellent 16-20	Very Good 11-15	Good 6-10	Needs Improvement 1-5
Introduction/ Thesis	exceptional introduction that grabs interest of reader and states topic. **thesis is exceptionally clear, arguable, well-developed, and a definitive statement	*proficient introduction that is interesting and states topic. **thesis is clear and arguable statement of position.	*basic introduction that states topic but lacks interest. **thesis is somewhat clear and arguable.	*weak or no introduction of topic. **paper's purpose is unclear/thesis is weak or missing.
Quality of Information/ Evidence	*paper is exceptionally researched, extremely detailed, and historically accurate. **information clearly relates to the thesis.	*information relates to the main topic. **paper is well-researched in detail and from a variety of sources.	*information relates to the main topic, few details and/or examples are given. **shows a limited variety of sources.	*information has little or nothing to do with the thesis. **information has weak or no connection to the thesis.
Support of Thesis/Analysis	*exceptionally critical, relevant and consistent connections made between evidence and thesis. **excellent analysis.	*consistent connections made between evidence and thesis **good analysis.	*some connections made between evidence and thesis. **some analysis.	*limited or no connections made between evidence and thesis. **lack of analysis.
Organization/ Development of Thesis	*exceptionally clear, logical, mature, and thorough development of thesis with excellent transitions between and	*clear and logical order that supports thesis with good transitions between and within paragraphs.	*somewhat clear and logical development with basic transitions between and within paragraphs.	*lacks development of ideas with weak or no transitions between and within paragraphs.

	within paragraphs.			
Conclusion	*excellent summary of topic with concluding ideas that impact reader. **introduces no new information.	*good summary of topic with clear concluding ideas. **introduces no new information.	*basic summary of topic with some final concluding ideas. **introduces no new information.	*lack of summary of topic.
Style/Voice	*style and voice are not only appropriate to the given audience and purpose, but also show originality and creativity. **word choice is specific, purposeful, dynamic and varied. ***sentences are clear, active (subject-verb-object), and to the point.	*style and voice appropriate to the given audience and purpose. **word choice is specific and purposeful, and somewhat varied throughout. ***sentences are mostly clear, active (SVO), and to the point.	*style and voice somewhat appropriate to given audience and purpose. **word choice is often unspecific, generic, redundant, and clichéd. ***sentences are somewhat unclear; excessive use of passive voice.	*style and voice inappropriate or do not address given audience, purpose, etc. **word choice is excessively redundant, clichéd, and unspecific. ***sentences are very unclear.
Grammar/Usage/ Mechanics	*control of grammar, usage, and mechanics. **almost entirely free of spelling, punctuation, and grammatical errors.	*may contain few spelling, punctuation, and grammar errors.	*contains several spelling, punctuation, and grammar errors which detract from the paper's readability.	*so many spelling, punctuation, and grammar errors that the paper cannot be understood.
Citation Format	*conforms to MLA/APA rules for formatting and citation of sources are perfect.	*conforms to MLA/APA rules for formatting and citation of sources with minor exceptions.	*frequent errors in MLA format.	*lack of MLA /APA format/numerous errors.
Works Cited/Bibliography	*entries entirely correct as to MLA/APA format.	*entries mostly correct as to MLA/APA format.	*frequent errors in MLA/APA format.	*lack of MLA /APA format; numerous errors.

Additional Comments:

Rubric for Presentation and Oral Defense

Criteria	Excellent presentation 15-20	Good presentation 8-14	Poor presentation 1-7
Introduction	contains a complete and well-organized overview statement.	Contains a complete but somewhat disorganized overview statement.	Provides no overview. statement or statement is so short as to be useless.
Completeness	addresses all required research guideline elements very well.	addresses most of the required research guideline. elements fairly well.	addresses few of the research guideline elements or does so poorly.
Organization	is well organized, moving from general topics to specific details; provides a good explanation of the work.	is somewhat disorganized and provides too much detail without giving a good explanation of the work.	is disorganized and deals completely with details without providing a broad explanation of the work.
Findings	student has made significant finding that are evidence base, accurate, and clearly expressed.	student has made few significant findings or finding is inconclusive.	student has made no significant findings and has not met objectives.
Technology	makes effective use of technology to find answer(s) to leading question(s).	makes improper use of technology to find answer(s) to leading question(s).	makes no use of technology to find answer(s) to leading question(s).
Speaking Skills	uses presentation resources as a guide, gives detailed explanations, is easily understandable, and keeps eye contact with the audience.	relies heavily on presentation to make report; somewhat comfortable with the topic.	essentially reads the material from a presentation to make the report; clearly uncomfortable with the topic.

Visual Aids	contains visual aides that help audience understand work; visuals have a neat and professional look, easily understood; used well to make points.	contains few or inadequate visual aids or visual aids have a neat and professional appearance, but poorly used in making points.	contains no visual aids or visual aids are so poorly constructed as to be worthless.
Questions and Answers	answers questions clearly and accurately.	answers only some of the questions well.	answers none of the answer questions well.

Additional Comments:

BIBLIOGRAPHY

Almeida, A. B., et al. (2016). *Research Fundamentals from Concept to Output: A Guide for Researcher and Thesis Writers.* Adriana Printing Co.

Anol, B. (2012). *Social Science Research: Principles, Methods and Practices.* Creative Commons Attribution-Noncommercial-Share Alike 3.0 Unpotted License.

Avilla, R. A. (2016). *Practical Research 1.* Diwa Learning System Inc.

Badke, W.B. (2012). *Teaching Research Process: The Faculty's Role in the Development of Skilled Students Researchers.* CP Chados Publishing.

Baraceros, E. L. (2019a). *Practical Research 1 2ⁿᵈ Edition.* Rex Book Store.

Baraceros, E. L. (2020b). *Practical Research 1 2ⁿᵈ Edition.* Rex Book Store.

Barrot, J. S. (2017a). *Practical Research 1 for Senior High School.* C & E Publishing, Inc.

Barrot, J. S. (2017b). *Practical Research 2 for Senior High School.* C & E Publishing, Inc.

Bermudo, P. J., et al. (2010). *Research Writing Made Simple: A Modular Approach for Collegiate and Graduate Students.* Mindshapes Corporation., Inc.

Calmorin, L. P., & Calmorin, M. A (2007). *Research Methods and Thesis Writing 2ⁿᵈ Edition.* Rex Book Store.

Calmorin L. P. (2010a). *Research and Statistics with Computer.* National Book Store.

Chico, A. M., & Matira, M D. (2016). *Practical Research for 21ˢᵗ Century Learners (Quantitative Research).* St. Augustine Publications, Inc.

Clemente, R, F., Julaton, AB., E. & Orleans, A. V. (2016). *Research in Daily Life 1* . Sibs Publishing House, Inc.

Creswell, J. W. (2005). *Educational research: Planning, conducting, and evaluating quantitative and qualitative research.* Pearson Education, Inc.

Cristobal, A. P., & Cristobal, MC. D.(2017a). *Practical Research 2 for Senior High School.* C & E Publishing, Inc.

Cristobal, A. P., & Cristobal, MC. D.(2017b). *Practical Research 1 for Senior High School.* C & E Publishing, Inc.

Dela Cruz, A. R. (2017). *Applications and Practice of Research for Senior High School: Inquiries, Investigations, and Immersion.* Phoenix Publishing House.

Dela Cruz, N. V. (2011). *A Guide to Thesis Writing.* Research and Publication Office St. Dominic Savio College.

Faltado, Ruben E. et al. (2016). ***Practical Research 2: Quantitative Research***. Lorimar Publishing, Inc.

Flores, M. F. (2016). ***Methods of Research in Business Education.*** Unlimited Books Library Services & Publishing Inc.

Garcia, C. D. (2003). ***Fundamentals of Research and Research Designing***. Katha Publishing Co., Inc.

Gay, L. R. et al. (2012). ***Educational Research: Competencies for Analysis and Applications.*** Pearson Education, Inc.

Gepila, E. C., et al. (2017). ***Research in Daily Life (Practical Research) 2: Introductory Guide to Quantitative Research***. Jenher Publishing House.

Jesson, J. (2011). ***Doing Your Literature Review: Traditional and Systematic Techniques***. Sage.

Institute for Academic Development (2021). ***Literature review***. University of Edinburgh. https://www.ed.ac.uk/institute-academic-development/study-hub/learning-resources/literature-review.

Lapan, s., Quartaroli, M., & Riemer, F. (2012). ***An Introduction to Research Methods and Designs***. Jossey-Bass, A Wiley Imprint.

Mc Bride, D. M. (2013). ***Process of Research in Psychology***. Sage.

Morgan, D. L. (2014). ***Integrating Qualitative and Quantitative Methods: A Pragmatic Approach***. Sage.

Ochave, Jesus A. et al. (1992). ***Research Methods***. Rex Book Store.

Pulmones, R. P. (2016). ***Quantitative Research***. Phoenix Publishing Inc.

Reyes, M. Z. (2004). ***Social Research: A Deductive Approach***. Rex Book Store.

Ridley, D. (2012). *The Literature Review: A Step-by-Step Guide for Students*. 2nd ed. Sage.

Samosa, R. C. (2020a). ***Understanding the End – to -End Praxis of Quantitative Research: From Scratch to Paper Presentation***. Book of Life Publishing.

Samosa, R. C. (2020b). ***Effectiveness of Claim, Evidence, and Reasoning as an Innovation to Develop Students' Scientific Argumentative Writing Skills.*** Unpublished Action Research. Department of Education, Region III, Schools Division of San Jose del Monte City, Bulacan.

Samosa, R. C et.al. (2021c). ***Practical Research 2: Quantitative Research*** . Beyond Books Publishing.

Samosa, R. C. (2021d). ***Cultivating Research Culture: Capacity Building Program Toward Initiatives to Improve Teachers Self-Efficacy , Research Anxiety and Research Attitude.*** Unpublished Action Research. Department of Education, Region III, Schools Division of San Jose del Monte City, Bulacan.

Samosa, R. C. (2021e). ***Cooperative Learning Approach as Innovation to Improve Students' Academic Achievement and Attitude in Teaching Biology.*** Journal of World Englishes and Educational Practices , 3(1), 01-10. https://doi.org/10.32996/jweep.2021.3.1.1.

Samosa, R. C. (2021f). ***CoSIM (Comics cum SIM): An Innovative Material in Teaching Biology.*** International Journal of Multidisciplinary Research Studies, 1 (1).

Serrano, A. C. (2016b). ***Practical Research 2: Quantative Research.*** Unlimited Books Library Services & Publishing Inc.

Trinidad, J. E. (2018a). ***Researching Philippine Realities.*** Ateneo De Manila University Press.

Trinidad, J. E. (2019b). ***Error – Proofing Your Research: Common Mistakes and How to Address Them.*** Ateneo De Manila University Press.

Braun, V. & Clarke, V. (2006): Using thematic analysis in psychology, Qualitative Research in Psychology, 3:2, 77-101. http://dx.doi.org/10.1191/1478088706qp063oa.

Young, F. C. (2002). ***Fundamental of Research Writing Made Simple.*** Bright Minds Publishing.

Zulueta, F. M., & Costales, NE B.(2003). ***Methods of Research, Thesis Writing and Applied Statistics.*** National Book Store.

ABOUT THE AUTHORS

RESTY SAMOSA, Ph.D

He is committed academician and researcher, brings his fervent passion for education to his roles as a faculty and guidance advocate at Cavite State University - Naic. Through his dedication, he actively contributes to molding the future generation of educators. He has taught courses in almost all facets of Natural Science, Research Methodologies, and Statistics in both basic education, tertiary and graduate levels.

He continues to contribute to academe as researcher, innovator, resource speaker, lecturer, thesis adviser, statistician, evaluator, demonstration teacher, and paper presenter at various seminars, conferences, and science fairs.

He also published several textbooks includes the following Understanding the End- to End Praxis of Quantitative Research: From Proposal to Paper Presentation, General Biology 1, General Biology 2, General Chemistry 1, General Chemistry 2, Practical Research 2: Quantitative Research, Practical Research 1: Qualitative Research, Inquiries, Investigation, and Immersion, How to Write and Publish Your Thesis? : Practical Guide for Students & Teachers and How to Write and Publish Your Dissertation, Exploring the Essence & Meaning from the Sound of Experiences: Qualitative Research, Fundamentals of Earth Science, From Proposal to Presentation: Demystifying Action Research Manual for Basic Education Teachers, Curriculum Design and Development for School Instruction: A Guide for Teachers, Project Assessments, and the Teacher and School Curriculum (A Reflective Guide).

In addition, he published research on high indexes international Journals; He also one of the Peer-Reviewers of the International Journal of Discoveries and Innovation in Applied Sciences, International Journal of Innovative Analyses and Emerging Technology, European Journal of Agricultural and Rural Education, International Review of Social Sciences Research, International Journal of Development and Public Policy and International Journal of Studies in Technology and Education.

He was the 2019 Action Research Champion in the 5th Division Research Congress for Teachers Category. He also won 2nd Outstanding Action Research Paper in the 7th Division Research Congress for Teachers Category in the DepEd, City of San Jose del Monte, Bulacan. He also bagged the 2021 Global Outstanding Teacher (Leadership in Education Academy & Development- Philippines), 2021 Global Leader Award in Excellence Leadership & Global Educators Award in Research (Beyond Books Publication), 2021 Outstanding Teacher (World Educators Leaders' Summit & Awards), 2021 Outstanding Teacher in Research (Educacio World), 2021 Best Speaker in the Research Intellectual Discussions (Institute of Industry and Academic Research Incorporated in partnership with Universiti Teknologi Mara in Thailand), 2021 Outstanding Educator of Philippine Association of Physics , Science Instructors and 2020 Outstanding Teacher in Research (DepEd CSJM, Bulacan) and 2022 Outstanding Learning Resource Developer (DepEd CSJM, Bulacan).

ELIZA MAE RODRIGUEZ – SAMOSA, MAEd

She is a graduate of Bulacan State University – Sarmiento Campus with the degree of Bachelor of Secondary Education major in Mathematics. Furthermore, armed with degree of Master of Arts in Education major Mathematics in Meycauayan College. Former College Faculty and Statistics Coordinator of Department of Biological and Physical Science of Cavite State University – Imus.

LAILANIE Q. DELA PEÑA, MEM., MAEd

Lailanie Q. Dela Peña earned her Bachelor's in Elementary Education and teaching license in 1999, laying the foundation for a remarkable career. With master's degrees in education management (PUP Open University) and Social Science (New Era University), she has become a dynamic educator. Currently a Grade 3 Special Science teacher, Lailanie has taught senior high and college students across English, education, social science, and research. A winning coach in journalism and the Festival of Talents, she composed a school hymn and presented action research at the 5th Division Research Congress in 2019. Her passion for research continues to shape her teaching and scholarly pursuits.